I0617320

RIO DE JANEIRO

The Spirit of Carnaval

FRANK PANCHO GONZALES

Copyright © 2025 **Frank Pancho Gonzales Publishing**

All rights reserved. No part of this publication may be reproduced, distributed, or transmitted in any form or by any means, including photocopying, recording, or other electronic or mechanical methods, without the prior written permission of the publisher, except in the case of brief quotations embodied in critical reviews and certain other noncommercial uses permitted by copyright law. For permission requests, write to the publisher, addressed "Attention: Book Rights and Permission," at the address below.

Published in the United States of America

ISBN 978-1-955243-06-3 (SC)
ISBN 979-8-89395-896-6 (HC)
ISBN 979-8-89395-897-3 (Ebook)

Library of Congress Control Number: 2025903869

Frank Pancho Gonzales Publishing
222 West 6th Street
Suite 400, San Pedro, CA, 90731
www.stellarliterary.com

Order Information and Rights Permission:

Quantity sales. Special discounts might be available on quantity purchases by corporations, associations, and others. For details, contact the publisher at the address above.

For Book Rights Adaptation and other Rights Permission.
Call us at toll-free 1-888-945-8513 or send us an email at admin@stellarliterary.com.

Contents

Joanie and Frank

Foreword

RIO

The very sound of the word alone conjures up vibrant, festive images of things I have heard and seen about the city! Long stretches of tropical sun drenched sandy beaches. Beautiful women on the beach in their skimpy "barely there" thong bikinis. Rich music *("The Girl from Ipanema" and samba)* that sets many a person into an immediate dancing frenzy. Savory heapings in the Churrascos of meats, fruits and vegetables that fill the nostrils with tantalizing aromas, and our stomachs eager to taste delicious foods. The giant statue of Jesus (Cristo Redentor) that overlooks the city, and that symbolizes Rio. The cable car trip traveling over a stretch of ocean to Sugarloaf Mountain. And, of course, Carnaval, called by many as the world's largest annual party. It increases in fervor each day for a week until it culminates the night before Ash Wednesday. I write of Carnaval with its Portuguese spelling; Portuguese is the official language of Brazil.

Since my high school years, I dreamed of travel to Brazil to experience the excitement and glitter of Carnaval. After getting married in 1978, I suggested this trip to my wife several times over the years. She did not share my interest in traveling either to Brazil, or to experience its closer cousin in New Orleans, the celebration of Mardi Gras.

In June, 2007, after a marriage separation, as I contemplated my future, I decided to start traveling to see places I had always dreamed of experiencing, even if I had to travel alone. My part time job as a backup bus driver for the senior apartments, where I now lived in retirement, could wait. As I sat around a campfire one cool August evening in 2007 with my friends, Shari and Mike, I talked about future travel sites and destinations in which I had an interest. I compared these with the destinations Shari and Mike also had an interest in seeing. Our first thoughts were of Mexico City and its surrounding areas including the Aztec pyramids. Mike and I both share an interest in world history and in cultural excursions.

As we contemplated our options, we decided to scrap our plans for Mexico City, since we had been there on previous trips. Instead, the time had come for something bolder, to visit a destination that captured our imaginations. We decided to make the trip of our past dreams, to go to Brazil for the upcoming celebration of Carnaval.

This celebration is reputed to be the "greatest show on Earth." Hundreds of thousands of tourists join the "cariocas" (e.g., Rio natives) for the five day frenzy of partying that culminates in the internationally acclaimed Sambadrome competitions among the 12 Samba schools (more of a description of this is in Chapter Seven with additional photos pages 100-109). The three of us had long desired to participate in the annual Carnaval celebration of Rio de Janeiro.

Rio now became the destination of choice. I told family and friends that I needed to make a pilgrimage to Rio so I could have something for which to repent in the upcoming season of Lent. Carnaval celebrates the excesses of life in anticipation of the penitence of Ash Wednesday, and Lent. I wanted to be in the middle of these excesses, savoring every drop.

By mid-September, 2007, Mike had already lined up the flights to Brazil, and an apartment rental in Rio. With these arrangements in place, I was ready to experience something I had heard about since my youth, and always dreamed of seeing in person. I was ready to make my pilgrimage to Cristo Redentor, to dance the Samba, and to enjoy Carnaval!

Acknowledgements

This trip would not have been possible without the determination of my friends, Mike and Shari. From the start, Mike took it upon himself to not only make the travel arrangements, but also to immerse himself in the customs and basic language of the Brazilian people. He performed hours upon hours of research using the internet to find points of interest. He bought books regarding Carnaval and the Sambadrome, purchased a Samba dance training DVD to prepare us for Samba dance moves, and many other things. Together with Shari, they drew up an itinerary that proved interesting, informative, and insightful for me.

I am grateful to my sister, Teri, and John, for their love and support in helping me to make this a most memorable trip.

I am especially thankful and grateful to my newly married wife, Annetta Joan, and to my family members Laura, Emily (and Justin, Olivia, Gabrielle, and Nathan), Alex (and Terrance), Kimberly (and Zoe and Sierra), Lynette (and Greg and Maggie), and Jason (and Shasta). Also, to mom (Josephine), Tony Sr. (and Barbara), Lupe (and Ron), Lou (and Joyce), Teri, Paul, and Mary Ann for their unending love and support, especially during those trying, difficult times for me after divorce.

I am appreciative to my son, Alex, and my daughter, Laura, for their assistance in editing this account.

I am very thankful to my friends, Elvia Martinez, and Johnny Jaime, and his wife, Julie. They have continued to shower me with their friendship and support, and, in particular, encouragement over the years for me to tell this story of my experiences in Rio.

I have the warmth and love of many friends from years past and the present, from the cities in Southern California of Yucaipa, Chino, Long Beach, Huntington Beach, Fountain Valley, Westminster, La Palma, Cerritos, Aliso Viejo, and in Denver, CO, and Morrill, NB. All of you have been, and continue to be, the wind beneath my wings.

To all of you I dedicate this account.

To all of you, thank you !

Chapter One

IVANA

Wednesday, January 30, 2008

Our long awaited trip to Rio de Janeiro finally started. Shari's daughter, Mary, dropped the three of us (Shari, Mike, and I) off at Los Angeles International Airport about 10:30 pm last night (Tuesday). There were no problems encountered at the check-in counter. We boarded the plane, and it departed on schedule at 1:00 am this morning.

The week before leaving on the trip, all of us developed colds. As luck would have it, my cold quickly progressed into pneumonia. When I visited the doctor, he advised me to postpone the trip, or skip it. With my medical history of serious respiratory illnesses, he told me point blank that my illness would be life threatening. He recommended an x-ray of my lungs to confirm his diagnosis of pneumonia. He thought that confirmation should then affect my decision about continuing on the trip.

But I told the doctor I was determined to make this trip, no matter what! To me, it was a once-in-a-lifetime opportunity. If I died making the trip it would be well worth it to me! Besides, I told him, I had already paid the airfare, had already prepaid my portion of the apartment rental, and made an advance payment for the Sambadrome ticket. Mike had set up our travel arrangements. We didn't have travel insurance with its refund clauses. The doctor asked me incredulously, "If I have the x-ray taken, and it confirms pneumonia, you are still going to make the trip?" I responded, "Hell, yeah!" The doctor replied, "And if I don't take the x-ray you are still going to make the trip?" Again, I responded, "Yes." He replied, "Well then, no use wasting an x-ray." Instead, he wrote me a prescription for Augmentin 875 mg, Doxycycline 100 mg, and MethylPred 4 mg, as well as a refill on all my other prescriptions.

Our itinerary to Rio de Janeiro, Brazil (also spelled "Brasil" in Portuguese and Spanish), would take us from Los Angeles International Airport over Mexico City to Panama City, Panama, a five hour flight. Panama City is in the same time zone as New York City. It is the main hub for flights between North America and South America. After a one hour layover in Panama City, we boarded a different flight to complete the loop to Rio, with an expected duration of seven more hour's flight time.

The flight to Rio from Panama City goes in a straight diagonal line over Medellin and Bogata, Colombia, over the entire stretch of the Amazon, to Brasilia (the capital of Brazil); then it curves down slightly to arrive in Rio.

By itself, Brazil appears to be the size of the continental USA, with maybe half of Alaska added in. The distance between Panama City to Mexico City, or to Miami, Florida, is about the same. It seemed odd to be flying into Panama City knowing it was the same time zone as New York City, which is three hours ahead of the Pacific Standard Time of California. But then Rio, still further to the right on the globe, is five time zones ahead of Pacific Standard Time. Our plane would be flying between 39,000 feet to 41,000 feet at a speed of approximately 489 mph.

Inside, our plane had six seats across, three on one side, three on the other, with a narrow aisle down the center of the plane all the way to the back. While the seats themselves were comfortable, the spacing of the seat area was cramped. I had requested an aisle seat because I have a large body frame (as much as I hate to admit it, I am overweight). This seating arrangement allows the top half of one side of my body to hang over into the aisle, leaving more room for the person who has to sit in the middle seat. The disadvantage of this seat is that a person is constantly being bumped by people and carts moving up and down the aisle.

There are some advantages, though, to sitting in the aisle seat. With the narrow aisles, sometimes the female (or an occasional male) passengers or flight attendants lose their balance and practically fall into your lap as they try to pass each other in the aisle on the way to the restrooms at either end of the plane cabin.

If I had observed someone's snotty or snobbish behavior earlier in the airport terminal or on the plane, I'd just as soon let that person fall to the floor rather than into my lap.

Another advantage to the aisle seat is that when the food cart stops close by, a person can sometimes reach over and help themselves to additional servings of whatever. I can get my drink, gulp it down, and ask the flight attendants for a refill before they can even move the cart away down the aisle. Or, sometimes I can reach over to get myself extra bags of peanuts, chips, etc. I always try to treat the flight attendants in a compassionate, understanding, humorous, and friendly manner. They, in turn, are often responsive to me, and allow me to help myself to the food cart (within reason).

On the second leg of the flight (from Panama City to Rio) our seats were at the front of the plane close behind First Class (one seat in row six, and two seats in row seven). I took the aisle seat in row six.

A young man named Manuel, possibly in his mid twenties, had the window seat in row seven next to Shari and Mike. He was gregarious, with an excited look to him. He planned to stay with friends in Niteroi, a city across the bay from Rio. He was originally from Venezuela, but was now living with his parents in Tampa, Florida. He was a civil engineering student at the University of South Florida. He was very easy to talk to, well mannered, and displayed an attitude of being studious. Shari thought that in the sea of eligible young bachelors, he would be a good catch for her unmarried adult daughter, Mary. Mike didn't seem as excited about him. Mike thought he should just throw Manuel back into the ocean of males and wait for a better fish for Mary.

Meanwhile, the two seats next to me stayed open. Finally, just minutes before take-off from Panama City, a very attractive young woman came aboard lugging a duffel bag that looked heavy and bulky. By the time she boarded, all the storage bins above us and around us were full, and most of the bin doors had been closed by the flight attendants. She looked very disconcerted about where she could store her bag. I noticed that when the people in First Class were boarding, the bin above aisle three (in First Class) was empty. That bin door though was now closed so its open space inside was not visible.

I called out to the woman that bin three had empty space. She disappointedly exclaimed, "But it's in First Class!" I shouted out in reply, "Other people behind me have put some of their things in First Class bins too" (which I had observed). She frantically kept opening bin doors up and down the aisle looking for an empty space before the plane doors closed for departure. Finally, she resigned herself to opening bin three in First Class. Sure enough, there was a huge open space right there in the middle of the bin. She heaved her heavy duffel bag up into the bin, and then came towards me. She had the window seat in my aisle. I stood up to let her in.

TIP: If you have bulky carry-ons, don't wait to be the last to board the plane.

During the early part of this flight, almost immediately she curled up in her seat and went to sleep. The flight was expected to take seven hours. Her clothing looked well worn, but not dirty. She was slightly unkempt. The drink cart came by, but since she was asleep, she missed her free drink. Then the flight attendants came again, this time handing out hot cloth towels for people with which to clean their hands in preparation for the dinner distribution.

She was still asleep, so she missed out on her hot towel. Finally, the food cart came. We were being given a choice between pork chunks in gravy (which tasted very good), or chicken in pasta noodles.

This time I decided to nudge her to see if she was hungry. I shook her shoulder gently, and woke her up. I told her, "I'm sorry to wake you, but I thought you might be hungry and the food cart is here." She was very grateful that I woke her up. She looked very dainty, and hungry. I mentioned that while she was asleep she had missed the drink cart and the hot cloth towels to clean her hands. I asked her if she wanted me to wake her anytime something was being handed out. She said "yes!"

Her name is Ivana. She was born in the Soviet Union, and her parents live in Moscow. As a student, she had moved to London to complete her PhD at Oxford University in corporate law. She was now a licensed solicitor (an attorney who practices corporate law; a "barrister" is an attorney who practices private law). She had become a naturalized citizen of the UK. Since she was born Russian, I asked her if she liked caviar.

She giggled, and said, "Of course I like caviar. My last name is "Sturgeon"" (the same as the fish that produces caviar).

Ivana is a wispy, long legged blonde. She is thirty five years old, and divorced. Her company in London had recently closed its operations in London to move them to Europe. But at this time she did not want to move with her company to Europe. She felt that in her career she would have more success in picking a job worldwide if she had a business master's degree from a US school such as Stanford, Harvard, or Yale. She told me that these three schools have an international reputation that would help her find a good job. In fact, she had already been advised that she was accepted to Stanford pending the completion of her application. But in her haste to commence her travel, she had inadvertently left out one item in her application. Now it was too late for her to return to London to find just that one item. She would have to miss the next semester at Stanford and wait for her chance again.

This trip, for Ivana, was part of a larger travel plan. She had already traveled to the Serengeti (Africa), she had scuba dived the Great Barrier Reef (Australia), seen Sydney (Australia), climbed the mountain trail to the sacred Inca city of Machu Picchu in the Andes Mountains (in Peru at about 14,000 feet), spent a week at the Galapagos Islands (Ecuador), and now on her way to Rio de Janeiro for Carnaval. After Rio, her plan was to continue to Buenos Aires (Argentina), and end with the Southern Cruise (of Antarctica) before returning to London to resume her business life, or enroll in one of the American universities mentioned previously.

Ivana was very easy to talk to. It helped that she thought I was smart and funny. I told her I admired her gumption in traveling alone on her worldwide trip. She told me she admired me for bravely making this journey, even though I was sick with pneumonia, and told by my doctor that this trip could be life threatening, and that I needed to cancel it.

We had enjoyable conversations throughout the remainder of the flight, talking about places in the world where she had already traveled and others she still wanted to see, and places I wanted to visit. My wish list for future travel included boating the Rhine River through

Transylvania and the Carpathian Mountains (the settings for the stories of Dracula, the wolf man, and Frankenstein), visiting Kiev and St. Petersburg, visiting Oslo (Norway), Copenhagen (Denmark), Berlin, Amsterdam, Greece, Istanbul, Nepal, Bangkok, Hong Kong, Beijing, Tokyo, Sydney (Australia), Auckland (New Zealand), Fuji, Bora Bora, Tahiti, the Galapagos Islands, and boating up the Amazon delta to observe piranha fish up close. Rio de Janeiro, and Carnaval, used to be on this list, but now was in the process of being fulfilled. I have already traveled to Mexico, Alaska and the major islands of Hawaii. The seven hour flight passed quickly!

We arrived at Galeao International Airport, Rio de Janeiro, Brazil, in the outskirts of the city on Wednesday night at 10:00 pm Rio time (five time zones ahead of my home in California). We departed the plane and walked down long, ugly brownish gray tunnels following the exit signs until we finally reached the baggage area.

Baggage areas in all the airports are the same. Bump - bump, bump - bump, bump - bump....luggage comes clomping down the conveyor line from the aircraft cargo hold. You would think that with all the various brands, makes, and colors of luggage, it should be easy to spot your own luggage. But no, all the luggage coming down the line seems to be the same color, and same size as mine. In fact, many of the luggage pieces look exactly the same. But, like usual, as each piece approached closer, it was not mine, nor the person next to me, nor the person next to them. Finally, someone would reach in to claim a piece. Ooopps, not their luggage, so back it would go on the conveyor. Waiting, waiting, waiting—suddenly, I spotted one luggage piece that looked like it could be mine. It came closer, closer, closer. YES, it was mine! With great joy I pulled it off the conveyor. Now I just had to wait with Shari and Mike for the rest of our luggage to come along.

TIP: Put colorful adhesive strips, or ribbons, on luggage handles or around luggage to help you recognize your luggage.

Finally, all our luggage pieces arrived. We had set up a special arrangement in advance for pick up from the airport and transport to our apartment. Ivana asked if she could share the same transportation we were using to get to her hotel, which, on our city map, was only a few blocks away from the apartment that we were renting. We didn't know how big the vehicle picking us up would be, or if the driver would even consider adding her. We explained this to Ivana, and she understood. Still, she stayed close by our side until it could be determined one way or another.

TIP: Know the address or cross streets of your hotel, or event you are attending.

Chapter Two

RIO

At Galeao airport, we passed through Customs with no problem after our entry card had been stamped. This card also serves as the exit card from Brazil. It was important that it be kept in a secure place. Finally, we came out to the general exit reception area. It was crowded with people waiting for their loved ones. Names were being yelled out, and some people were holding signs with the names of someone unknown to them but whom they needed to pick up. In the middle of the crowd I spotted a sign with a name in big bold blue letters, "Michael Row." I loudly called out this name, and pointed to the man holding the sign. He immediately made his way to the mouth of the exit area from where the passengers were leaving.

Even though it was 10:00 pm, the weather outside the airport terminal was oppressively hot and humid! As we met our driver, Mike pointed to him and immediately questioned, "(Are you) Lamborghini?" (the man who is to be our contact for whatever we need in Rio). The man shook his head, "no." We tried asking him in English and Spanish if he had room for one more passenger, but he didn't understand our question (as we found throughout our trip, Brazilians did not seem to make an effort to speak anything other than Portuguese). So we resorted to using sign language – one finger pointing to Mike, then Shari, then me, then one finger pointing to Ivana. This time he understood, and nodded, "yes." Sign language was to be our universal language during this trip whenever we got stuck trying to make our questions known.

TIP: When using sign language, make sure the outcome meets or satisfies your intended message.

We followed the driver to his vehicle. It was one of those tall, metallic colored Mercedes Benz passenger vans, the Sprinter BlueTec model, which, at that time, was uncommon to see in the USA. It had room for up to fifteen passengers (without luggage).

We settled into the comfort of an air conditioned van. In leaving the airport, the van weaved its way with ease through traffic. It appeared we were picked up on the third level of the airport structure. We exited the airport and found ourselves being driven through an industrial part of town.

Suddenly, after about twenty minutes, the surroundings changed and we emerged into a residential area with tall apartment buildings. It was now about 10:45 pm. In the darkness, with the occasional street lamp and the car lights of oncoming traffic, we were astounded to see a city that looked like a huge slum with heaping piles of trash at the curbs, and overflowing into the streets. We passed pile after pile of stacked up rubbish and trash at various places on the streets outside of buildings. Then, out of nowhere, a trash truck appeared in front of us; it was stopped, and collecting trash. Wouldn't you know it! We arrived on trash pickup night! Yes, the trash pickup was being performed at night.

Finally, the van stopped. Our apartment was in Copacabana, in a darkened part of the downtown area on the main street. The driver dropped us off first. He charged us thirty US dollars per passenger. He pointed to small glass door in the wall of seamless buildings. It was the entryway into our apartment complex. Then he took Ivana to her hotel.

After unloading our luggage from the van, Mike tapped on the glass door with his fist, and a uniformed man came forward down an inside hallway towards the door. As he opened the door, Mike asked him in a questioning voice, "Lamborghini?" The man shook his head, "no," but he let us in.

As we entered the hallway lobby, a bald headed slender man, dressed in a futbol (soccer) shirt and shorts suddenly appeared. He was Lamborghini. He was in his fifties, about 5'7" tall, spoke very good English, and was accompanied by a younger, pretty woman whom we assumed was his girlfriend. He led us to the "social elevator" (a.k.a., the fancy elevator), and pressed the button selection for the fifth floor. However, because the social elevator only held about four people without luggage, we had to split ourselves into two groups. Lamborghini went up with Shari, Mike, and some of our luggage; upon the return of the elevator, I followed with Lamborghini's girlfriend and the rest of the luggage.

When the "social elevator" door opened on the fifth floor, the lobby there had an open standing space of about 6' X 4'. The fifth floor lobby served only two apartments (ours being one of the two). Because the lobby was small, there was not a lot of room to maneuver in it. When there were three people in the elevator, and they all exited on the same floor, the door of the elevator sometimes could not close easily. If the lobby was crowded, someone either had to move closer to another person, or closer to the lobby wall, to allow the elevator door to close completely behind them, and thus be available for usage by others waiting to use the elevator. In essence, the elevator door opened right to the front door of the apartment.

Later on we found out that the "service elevator" (e.g., that elevator that was plain and ugly) in the rear of the building was slightly larger in size, but reserved for use by the domestic help, or for those coming back full of sand from the beach, which is only two blocks away.

The interior of the apartment was decorated in a luxurious and opulent style, with imported Grecian style tile on the walls and bathrooms, and porcelain sinks. The TV and stereo's in the bedrooms were compact and modern. The apartment looked like a miniature French style Versailles palace for munchkins (the small people from the "Wizard of Oz" movie) because everything was sized for small people in a cramped setting, with a small entry way, a small kitchen, a small bathroom, and reduced height doorways to the various rooms.

By now it was about 11:30 pm Wednesday evening. We were starving! The last food on the plane was served about three hours earlier, but it was only a heated flat bread with a slice of ham and melted cheese. It looked and tasted like a croissant someone had stepped on, then served to us to eat (this time, Ivana was awake and eager for her snack). Lamborghini indicated that there was a restaurant just across the street that was still open, and a grocery store about two blocks down the street.

We crossed the street to the restaurant (a "kilograma"), which still had its lights on, but a man wearing a suit was turning people away, saying, "fechada" (e.g., "closed"). We went looking for the grocery store; it too was closed. All the stores were closed, or closing.

One street corner had a pharmacy that appeared to be still open. Through the windows we could see shelves inside with bottled water and snacks. We went in and bought several bottles of water and some snacks. The main cash register had developed a problem; we waited while the attendants went into the back room to add up charges using an alternate method.

TIP: Carry snacks for long plane flights or late-in-the-day arrivals.

As we returned to the apartment, we noticed what appeared to be a coffee shop, named, in English, "The Winner." It had a flashing sign indicating "24 Horas" (in Spanish meaning "open 24 hours"). The window display unit, as seen from the sidewalk, showed croissants and muffins. We went inside, thinking we would just pick up coffee and croissants to hold us over until the morning. However, once inside, all the display cases were completely empty. A menu was printed on the wall; we asked if there were sandwiches available we could buy. Again, no one understood our questions in English or our Spanish.

Then, one of the waiters, with a white apron around his waist, approached us. He was a handsome, but sheepish looking, shy young man; he brought us a menu. He was maybe eighteen or nineteen years of age, broad shouldered with long arms and big hands. He was thin at his waist, and had dark brown tanned skin. He motioned for us to sit at a table, then he left momentarily.

Although all the entrées on the menu were listed in Portuguese, some of the words were similar to Spanish and English. The menu showed pictures of hors d'oeuvres, sandwiches, tortas, and pizza. The menu listed a variety of drinks with their names in English (e.g., Manhattan, Irish whiskey, Rum & Coke, etc), and wines and other refreshments, which we did not recognize, with their names in Portuguese.

When the waiter returned, we pointed to the entrées on the menu we thought we might enjoy. With our fingers, we indicated two large pizzas, one of four cheeses and the other Neapolitan (which, when it arrived, meant a cheese pizza with a large slice of tomato baked on top of it). I pointed to the drink portion of the menu and asked for cerveza (the Spanish word for beer). The waiter looked confused.

He did not recognize my Spanish word (in Portuguese the word is "cerveja"). I pointed instead to a drink listed as "seca." The waiter asked me, "piña, naranha, o fresa?" (in Spanish, pineapple, orange, or strawberry). This meant I was pointing to the fruit drink section of the menu. I pointed to a different listing in the drink section. It indicated, "Skol." That seemed that maybe it could be beer. The waiter asked me, "vaso larga o vaso corto?" This sounded like he was asking if I wanted a large glass, or small glass. I replied, "larga." Mike asked for decaffeinated coffee, and also said, "larga," pointing to himself. Shari pointed to the listing on the menu indicated as "Irish Coffee," then pointed to herself also asking for it as a decaf coffee. I did sign language indicating I wanted an Irish Coffee too, in case my vaso larga was not beer but something different. The waiter looked at me, questioning with his eyebrows and hands, "You want both?" I nodded "yes." He brought the Skol first, which were two long neck bottles of Brazilian Skol beer chilled in a bucket of ice. The waiter opened one bottle, then poured about three inches into a glass for me, then the same into a glass for Mike (upon entering the coffee shop, we noticed the locals drinking their beer from a glass, not directly from the bottle or can).

Mike and I toasted each other, "Skol," and took a sip. It was delicious! Shari, who is not a beer drinker, asked if she could try it. She took a sip from Mike's glass and immediately said, "Ummm, that's good!" A few moments later, the waiter reappeared, saying something to the effect that they were out of decaf coffee and Irish coffee. He asked Shari if she wanted seca, expecting her to say one of the three types of fruit drinks he had previously mentioned. But Shari shook her head, pointed to herself, and said "Skol." The waiter looked at her incredulously, asking her again if she wanted seca, or Skol. But Shari shook her head and her finger with the motion, "no," then saying loudly and clearly "Skol," and pointing to herself. The waiter brought her a glass, and added another beer to the bucket. He poured her about three inches of beer.

After a short wait, the waiter brought out the pizzas. They were thin crust, but tasty, pizzas. He cut a slice and put it on Shari's plate; then, he did the same for Mike and I. He poured more beer into our glasses.

As we finished a slice of pizza on our plate, he would look to see which pizza we indicated we wanted for the next slice, and so on; he was very attentive to our needs. He did the same with the beer. When he brought the beer initially for Shari, I indicated with my fingers to bring two more beers. As a beer bottle would finish, he would bring another bottle and nestle it into the ice in the bucket. As the beer level in each glass lowered, he would pour a little more beer in to keep the glass more or less at the same level as before. He hovered around the table to see when a pizza slice or more beer was needed. Finally, we were full. We had eaten close to one and a half pizzas, and drank, between the three of us, about twelve bottles of Skol beer.

All this time our waiter had stayed most attentive to us, making sure that we were satisfied, giving us his full attention, being as helpful as he could to obvious travel-weary tourists, and making us feel welcome in his restaurant and in his city.

Chapter Three

KILOGRAMA

Thursday, January 31, 2008

We returned to the apartment by 2:00 am (Thursda`y) morning, and tried to go to sleep. We kept trying, without success, to fall asleep. Our apartment was located on a main street of Rio, and the noise outside was deafening in spite of this late hour of night. The noise continued all throughout the remainder of the night. It was the noise of the car tires on the street, car horns, constant traffic, the diesel noise of the buses, and the people talking loudly to each other as they walked on the sidewalk outside.

Then I heard what sounded like a loud, violent argument outside. It was a couple standing in front of a store across the street facing each other and shouting angrily at each other. I looked out the window to watch the action. The man had something long and pointed in his hand that looked like a knife. The woman was holding a bottle in her hand, and waving it in a motion suggesting she was ready to hit the man with it. As I watched, the man and woman came closer and closer, he with the knife still up in the air, and she with the bottle still in her hand. They went from being about five feet apart to coming within an arm's length of each other, still arguing loudly with each other. As a stranger to the city, I was not about to try to intervene. I didn't know how to contact the authorities, or what to do. I was also five stories up from the street level, in a building with a slow elevator, and no way to get back into the building once the outside door closed. When I saw how close they had gotten to each other, still arguing and waving their weapons, but neither backing off, I figured it was just a lover's quarrel. I decided not to continue watching, but to try to sleep. Next morning I looked out to see if there was a body, or blood, on the sidewalk… nope, no body, no blood.

Good thing I went back to sleep, rather than waiting to witness something exciting, or sickening, to happen.

As we would recount to each other later in the day, none of us could sleep soundly through the night. We would remain asleep only short periods of time. The noise outside our windows would waken us. We would fall back asleep, wake up again with the noise, fall asleep, and so on and so on. This pattern of waking, then falling back asleep, continued throughout the late morning into the afternoon. Finally, at about 7:00 pm, all three of us were awake at the same time, and hungry. We decided that we should eat first, then go buy groceries. Just across the street from our apartment was the kilograma, where we had tried to eat the night before.

A kilograma is a type of restaurant where you can pay for a flat rate sit down meal; or, go through the buffet line, make food selections, have your plate weighed, and be charged by the kilogram. A person is allowed to return to the buffet as many times as they want. Upon entering, we were each handed a card that resembled a credit card in size and look. This acted as our ID for the buffet line and the weighing of our food.

We were shown to a table, but didn't know how to proceed from there since this was our first time in a kilograma (as well as being in a different country with possibly different customs for eating in a buffet). Our waiter, Bernicio, acted like he understood my inquiry (in Spanish) about how to proceed, but he responded to me in Portuguese (which can sound like Spanish, but is different). He wrote two prices on the table covering made of butcher type paper. We thought at first that one price was for beverages and the other for the food. Later, we figured out that the prices indicated the flat rate cost of the meal verses the price per kilogram. However, Bernicio's hand motions were really all the instruction that we needed, so we headed towards the buffet line.

The buffet was very similar to our buffets here. You picked up a clean plate, walked around looking at the various offerings, decided what you wanted, and put that on your plate in the proportions you wanted. Then you walked to the cashier, who weighed the plate, and gave you a printed ticket with the weight of the food and the cost.

The cashier gave you your silverware sealed in a plastic baggie, and you returned to your table with your food. Drinks and water were available at an additional cost. If you were still hungry, and wanted additional servings of whatever, you just picked up a clean plate, selected the entrees you wanted, gave the previous ticket to the cashier, and a new total was added as a separate entry to the old total on a new receipt.

The food entrees looked very similar to the typical salad and food bars here in the USA. Offerings included vegetable salads (I could not identify some of the vegetables), egg salad, fruit salads, a pasta style station with noodles and what appeared to be "lasagna," a meat station (with filè mignon and other cuts of meat that I didn't recognize), a seafood station with salmon, fried fish (and other unrecognizable sea creatures), a cheese and salami station, hot grilled meats of various types (that looked like beef, pork, and chicken), and last, but not least, a fully stocked dessert station.

In every menu I saw in Rio, one meat entrée was always listed and identifiable to me in its Portuguese spelling – filè mignon. In Brazil, filè mignon is as common as hamburger meat is in the USA. It is not expensively priced; it's usually in the mid price range. Needless to say, from this point on, I always knew I had a backup meat I recognized that I could order when needed.

The waiter asked what we wanted to drink. We ordered a bottle of water for each of us; bottled water is never free. We also requested a bottle of red wine; the wine had a smooth taste and was delicious.

When we were full, and ready to leave, the waiter picked up our payment, which was made using a credit card (upon entry to the kilograma the credit card symbols of Mastercard, Visa, etc. were visible on the front door). After subtracting the cost of the drinks, we discovered that paying by the weight had been cheaper for us than paying the flat rate for the food.

TIP: Look for, and use, credit cards whenever possible. Often, local vendors cannot return exact change for US currency, and you end up overpaying. Or, use local currency.

With full stomachs, we moved on to the task of grocery shopping at the local market about two blocks away. This grocery store was part of a chain of grocery stores of the same name that are all set up internally in the exact manner. Once you learned the layout of one store, all the others follow the same pattern.

The grocery store had all the major things you would expect, but their emphasis on packaging and store layout was very different from our ideas in the USA of how things should be. For example, the stores were small and cramped. The aisles were narrow. There were big selections of some things (such as toothpaste), and small selections of other things (such as hand soap and laundry soap). The stores did not carry toys, stationery items, greeting cards, flowers, gardening tools, plastic ware, or automotive items.

The stores offered a selection of sandwich style breads, sweet breads (including Mike's "must have" coconut bread), dairy, paper goods, fresh and packaged meats, fresh fruits, and a wide selection of liquors and beers.

The fresh cheese station had a tall mound of varieties of cheeses all stacked up and labeled. The cheeses were packaged in casings, much like fresh sausage. When a cheese was picked up to identify its type, a slimy film was left on your fingers; there were no paper towels in sight with which to wipe your hands.

Milk was not refrigerated; instead, it had a preservative added and was sold in small cardboard rectangular boxes left out on the open shelf. (On a later trip to the grocery store, a tourist looking for fresh milk asked me if I knew where he could find it. I showed him. He made a disgusted face. Then he asked a store clerk, who also showed him the same location. The tourist ended up leaving without buying milk. I think he was looking for milk that was refrigerated).

Eggs were hard to buy; it was a selection of either fresh eggs or packaged (e.g., wrapped in plastic) eggs. After our first purchase of fresh eggs, we later found that these eggs were not fresh; the contents were rotting inside the shell. Of course, you didn't discover this until the egg was cracked for cooking. The "good eggs" to buy, that were similar to our accustomed tastes, were those that were packaged.

All in all, the grocery stores were easy to shop because the pictures on the outside wrappings on all items showed you exactly what the contents were. Identification was made easy for the consumer and tourist, even if the writing on the label was in Portuguese.

The checkout cash register area was small and cramped. The grocery carts were less than half the size of our grocery carts here in the USA. As I moved through the narrow aisles pushing my cart I felt like I was driving a mini racing car through an obstacle course.

When we exited the store with our proud belongings of food, a thin, bare-chested boy of about thirteen years old came up to me holding out the palm of one hand and motioning the other hand to his mouth.

He asked me something in Portuguese, but the meaning to me was clear. He was asking for a donation of money for food. I had been expecting requests for handouts because this practice was common no matter where you traveled. It's also common that people begging for donations did it as a profession, and particularly targeted tourists.

TIP: Carry local coinage and/or small paper currency for when donations are requested.

I had prepared myself for donation requests by having a handful of Brazilian coins ready in my pocket. This way, in the event I was asked for a donation, I wouldn't have to pull out my wallet and give a bigger donation than I wanted, as well as being able to keep my cash hidden and secure. I reached into my pocket, and pulled out the smallest coin I could feel, probably a ten centavos Brazilian coin (maybe five cents US). I placed the coin in the boy's hand, and then continued walking back to the apartment.

But the boy made a loud exclamation. He came up around me to face me again. He gave me his pleading eyes routine, motioning to the coin in his hand that I had just given him, then to his mouth. The meaning was clear. "Only ten centavos? Can't you give me more?" I shrugged my shoulders, and kept on walking. Again the boy came up around me and faced me. This time he gave me the motion of his hand under his elbow, jerking it upwards. It is the international sign of calling someone a cheapskate. Then the boy held out his hand again. This time I pointed to the coin in his hand, then to my own open palm. I told him in Spanish, "If you don't want it, I do," pointing for him to move the coin from his hand to my hand. And I kept on walking. Again the boy came up around me with his hand open. Again I told him in Spanish, "If you don't want it, I do," and I made the same hand motions as before. The boy grabbed my hand, opened it, and put all the change he hd in his own pockets into my hand, saying something to the effect of, "Here, you take it! You probably need it more than me!" I responded in English, "Thank you."

Holding his money tightly in my hand, I put my hand into my pants pocket, then continued walking away. A few moments passed. In a blur, the boy was in front of me again, with tearful eyes, pleading, and saying something unmistakable to the effect of, "My money, my money. I want my money. Please give me my money back!"

I still had my hand in my pants pocket tightly around the coins he had put into my hand, so I just pulled my hand out and gave him back all the coins he had given me. In a flash he was gone.

Throughout the remainder of the trip, Shari and Mike referred to this incident as "when Pancho out begged the beggar" (many years prior to this trip, I had earned the nickname of "Shafty" (e.g., giving someone the "shaft") when I would be asked at work to make monetary donations towards some cause that was not important to me. I was not known for being overly generous in these instances).

Several days later, a similar incident of "out-begging the beggar" occurred to Mike as he exited the same grocery store. It may have even been the same boy. But Mike thought to himself, "I'll do what Pancho did. It worked for him, so it should work for me." Mike took the same exact approach. After several attempts to get more money from him, the boy gave up and went looking elsewhere for better prospects.

That night, we had a lightning and thunder storm with strong gusty winds. It was exciting to watch the lightning bolts continuously light up the sky, with rain showers drenching the street below, and watching from the window as people outside scampered for cover.

Chapter Four

THE KNIGHTHOOD OF SIR MICHAEL

Friday, February 1, 2008

Today we woke up to a beautiful, sunny morning. Our plan was to visit Cristo Redentor, the giant monument of Christ the Redeemer that is currently considered to be one of the seven manmade wonders of the world. It overlooks the city of Rio and the bay. Then, if time and energy allowed, we would travel across the city in the afternoon to Sugarloaf Mountain, another famous Rio landmark.

After a small breakfast of coffee, toast, and fruit salad, we started out around 8:45 am for the subway that would take us to an intersection where we could catch a city bus to the monument of Cristo Redentor. This gave us an opportunity to see some of the city.

I have been very impressed with the public transportation here in Rio. There seemed to be hundreds of buses passing us on the street. So far I have not seen one bus so full that people were forced to hang out of the entrance/exit doorways, or stand tightly packed in the center aisle of the bus. At times, the subways were crowded, but the people were not stacked in on top of each other. This was true even when passengers were traveling with overflowing pieces of costuming that they would be using later in the day for the Sambadrome or for a street parade. This indicated to me that there was an abundance of public transportation, because even with the influx of crowds and tourists for the major holiday, public transportation could handle it.

Unfortunately, there was one major inconvenience to me in the public transportation. It was the turnstiles. Every bus had one, and every subway platform as well. On the buses, the driver did not collect the fare. Turnstiles were located on the center aisle just behind the driver. There was someone seated in the area across from the driver to whom the fare must be paid. After payment had been made, this bus employee released a brake allowing the turnstile to cycle. A passenger wanting to board the bus stepped up into the bus past the driver, stopped at the turnstile to pay the fare, then, after paying, was allowed admission into the bus seating area.

Where this presented me a problem was that I am larger in weight and body frame than most Brazilians.

While I could fit into the turnstile turned sideways, my body and my backpack would get stuck in the turnstile when it reached its midpoint in cycling. Meanwhile, other passengers waiting behind me would get impatient as they waited to also pass through to get to their seats.

I finally found a way to move through the turnstile smoothly. I had to lift my backpack up, and stand on my tip toes so that the center of my butt was just above the turnstile arm. This would create enough clearance for me to pass cleanly through the turnstile. It took some time for me to get the pattern down. I don't think Shari or Mike realized I kept getting stuck in the turnstiles, since they were always ahead of me.

We reached the street level admission area of Cristo Redentor at about 9:45 am. Since this world renown monument is a "must see" in Rio, it is always crowded with tourists and pilgrims. Every twenty minutes, a two car tram goes up to a station close to the top of the mountain (the monument of Cristo Redentor is at the top), while another two car tram returns from that drop off location. Our tram ticket was scheduled for 11:00 am; we had to wait.

Street level tram station

Waiting for the tram

We visited the shops, then settled into a crowd of people already standing in line waiting for their scheduled tram. This way we thought we would be close to the front of the line for when our tram came. As the group scheduled for 10:40 am boarded, we were left positioned right at the front of the line for the 11:00 am boarding. But, as is typical everywhere, people slowly materialized to the side of us, then slowly but surely edged us out to be in front of us. It didn't matter; when it came time for us to board, there were still plenty of good seats available.

Mike had found out from his pre-trip studies of Rio that on the tram ride up the mountain the best seats are on the right side of the tram. This was the side we settled into. It afforded us some of the most impressive views of the city of Rio, and the bay, on our way up. The left side view was mainly the side of the mountain, consisting of rain forest jungle foliage of giant trees, ferns, vines, etc. About every half mile on the way up were lifelike and life size color painted statues of saints, animals, birds, indigenous hunters, etc, so it was an interesting ride for the tram passengers sitting on either side.

View of Rio

The tram took us up the high mountain on a ride that lasted about twenty minutes. After that, there still remained a climb to get to the escalator that ends at the entrance of Cristo Redentor.

The escalator was the final step in gaining access to Cristo Redentor. People could take either an elevator to that escalator, or climb more than two hundred stairs to get to the escalator.

An infectious Carnaval atmosphere – "Let the festivities begin!"

The waiting line for the elevator was enormous. Mike was sure that the escalator was just a few steps up and around the side of the mountain. He convinced us to walk around and climb the stairs. In the oppressive heat (of what felt like more than one hundred degrees) and humidity, we needed to take several breaks to catch our breath and sip cool water. About three fourths of the way up there was a small café where we stopped to rest and have a beer to celebrate our pilgrimage there..

View from café

Finally, we made it to the point where the elevator ended, and the escalator started. Up the escalator we went, until we were finally at the monument of Cristo Redento.

When I am talking about oppressive heat, I had no way to determine if the temperature was in the low or high one hundred degrees. It might have been two hundred degrees. Tourists were "pink" from sun exposure.

TIP: On each day of your trip, pack sun block and lip balm.

The throng of people already at the monument was immense, with people packed into a concrete platform at the top of the mountain peak to see this huge statue of Christ with outstretched arms facing the city. In my estimation, the platform could hold about three hundred people. There was much elbowing going on as people tried to get around each other, jostling for a better angle to take their photos. In one corner, there appeared to be a Catholic mass service being said, with a priest in vestments and altar servers. In another corner, the rosary was being recited by a group of nuns and pilgrims in what sounded like the Portuguese language. In another corner, devotions were being held. And in between, and around all these religious activities, tourists were snapping pictures and climbing on the concrete wall sidings to get a picture of themselves with the giant statue of Christ in the background, or a photo of the city below.

To get these photos, they would inadvertently knock other people off balance and out of the way as they inched along trying to find better viewing spots of the city and the bay below. Photographers were even lying flat on the ground trying to get a photo shot of the complete statue from the feet to the top of the head. Of course, not being easily visible in the tight throng of tourists, sometimes someone would step on them, or trip on them. People everywhere were getting their photo taken, then retaken because someone else blocked their picture at the last minute by passing in front of the camera. It was like being in a zoo atmosphere!

Finally, we felt we had experienced enough chaos. We returned to the top tram platform for the ride to take us back down the mountain. The ride down was memorable only because when the tram was moving, the air felt cooler. When we reached the street level, it was the early afternoon. We still had time to fit in the excursion to Sugarloaf island/mountain, in the bay offshore from Rio. We started out towards that destination. Later we would find out this was a good decision. Each remaining day of the trip it rained.

The afternoon weather in Rio continued to be hot and humid. Just being outside of any air conditioned room caused our clothing to droop from dampness and sweat. I would find that even carrying a change of clothing in my backpack would not be enough. You could change clothes ten times in an hour, and the clothing would still be damp from perspiration. Later I also found, from experience, that if I forgot to remove the damp clothing, or even dry clothing, from my back pack upon return to the apartment, it would soon develop a musty odor that did not easily go away. After showering, moments later our skin would again be wet with perspiration. Sweat would drip from our hair onto our shoulders.

There was something else very noticeable. Few of the people we came into contact with had a smell of body odor. The few people that had noticeable body odor appeared to be men from Europe, or maybe SOUTH ASIA. We could be standing like blades of grass, pressed together in a space, like in a cable car, a restaurant, or an elevator, and still no smell of body odor. Also, very few people wore cologne, or perfume. What you could smell was sun block lotion, or musty clothing.

I noticed that in Rio very few men spit, including tourists. In fact, during our total of nine days in Rio, I only witnessed one homeless man, and one woman, spitting. With my pneumonia, I was often coughing up chunks of phlegm that needed to be expelled, but I would usually put them into a paper tissue for disposal.

TIP: Carry extra paper tissues.

While we were walking towards the cable car system that would get us to Sugarloaf, in the Urca section of town, I coughed up a sizeable chunk of phlegm. I did not have any paper tissue, and was about to spit it out into the bushes when I realized that we were in front of the naval academy. The bushes were on naval property. Uniformed armed guards were standing watch outside the building. I decided not to start an international incident, or get shot, or get thrown into jail, for defacement of government property; I didn't spit. I didn't want my actions to be misinterpreted.

Sugarloaf is another internationally well known and visited tourist spot of Rio. It was a huge chunk of mountain that rises up out of the sea in two pieces. The usual way to reach it from the mainland was a cable car ride from the mainland over the water to the first peak, then another cable car from the first peak over the water to the second peak. It offered tremendous and spectacular views of Rio, the surrounding islands, and, in the distance, Cristo Redentor. The Sugarloaf cable car start was located within the confines of a Brazilian naval base in Urca. In addition to the naval academy building, the navy had a private beach, and officers club, in Urca.

The cable car system was located adjacent to the officers club, where two restaurants were open to the public. We were hungry; we decided to have lunch at one of the restaurants. In one, food was served in a buffet style, while in the other, a sit down menu was offered. We asked if we could look at the buffet to see what was being served. It did not look at all appetizing. We had arrived at a time the lunch menu was beginning to transition to the dinner menu, which was still a half an hour away. We would be scrapping the bottom of the barrel in many containers of food, and it seemed that the food was not about to be replenished. We went instead to the sit down restaurant. It was here that Mike earned his knighthood (from me).

We were sitting at a round table on the outside patio facing the ocean waiting for our food that we had already ordered. We were separated from the beach sand by a concrete sea wall.

Two sizeable overweight women (at least by Brazilian standards) were sitting at a table next to us. The woman closest to us was acting in a snobbish manner, like she felt she was important, towards the waiter, flashing her military ID card and demanding or complaining loudly about something; she was speaking in Portuguese so I didn't know what her complaint was about.

During a lull in her remonstrations we noticed a huge black ant crawling towards her along the top of the sea wall that separated the dining area from the beach. We estimated the black ant to be close to two inches long. It may have been a legendary and dreaded "Brazilian army ant" scout (belonging to a species feared for being aggressive, ravenous, and predatory) looking for food, or maybe it was a Brazilian "Navy" ant (because it was on naval territory), or maybe a miniscule Komodo dragon. But whatever it was, it was BIG.

It was crawling towards the woman closest to us, the one acting very snobbish. Her luncheon partner noticed it, and screamed out for her friend to move. As soon as she saw it, the snobbish woman became hysterical. She tried feverishly to brush the critter off the sea wall with her cardboard glass coaster. But to no avail. The creature held firm; it would not dislodge from the wall. The woman became more frantic and hysterical, screaming in fright as she tried to shove the ant away from her. She looked so frightened and pitiful that finally Mike gallantly came to her rescue. He took his napkin, and smote the dragon......er, the ant, whatever. Both women looked so grateful and adoringly to Mike for his gallantry. For his selfless actions in the face of great danger, with no thought to his own personal safety, Mike was knighted by me as "A Knight of the Round Table." I told him, "Kneel, Michael, Lord of the Flies, Earl of Insects, Duke of It Out." He knelt at the table.

I tapped both his shoulders with my dinner knife and said, "Rise, Sir Michael, Lord of the Flies, Earl of Insects, Duke of It Out, Slayer of Dragons, and Defender of Overweight Vestal Virgins." Then Sir Michael rose, and took his rightful place as a Knight of our Round Table to finish his meal.

Good thing he was knighted, because within minutes, a second large black creature, about the same size, appeared. Immediately, the two women turned to Sir Michael, screaming and imploring his intercession. But Sir Michael did not need to do anything this time. In turning to ask for his assistance, the snobbish woman moved so far back in her chair that her butt came down on top of the ant, and squashed it. And since she could no longer see it, she calmed down, thinking that Sir Michael had again saved the day by killing the ant, or that he had knocked it to the ground and it had wandered off. In her mind, Sir Michael came to her rescue a second time, even though he was relieved of having to slay a second dragon… er, ant, or whatever.

In spite of the ant incident, our meal was most delicious. Sir Michael had ordered Tornedos of Beef with small, round potatoes; Shari had ordered a chicken fried steak covered with pureed potato parmesan (mmm, it was tasty!). I had ordered filete Oswaldo with fries and some kind of tree or plant root dressing.

After lunch, we took the cable car up to the first Sugarloaf peak.

We spent about forty five minutes admiring the view, and then took the second cable car up to the next peak. The view from both peaks is absolutely spectacular and stunning.

Cristo Redentor (center of photo) from Sugarloaf peak

Ipanema Beach (view from Sugarloaf)

After about an hour at the second peak, we descended Sugarloaf and returned to the apartment feeling worn out.

I have noticed that the streets of Rio were filled with small vehicles. Most of the cars were European made, such as Peugeot, Fiat, Audi, VW, SAAB, Mercedes Benz, Renault, Citroën, and a some Ford and Chevy models. There were no Japanese or Korean made cars (later, in Panama City, we noticed the exact opposite. In Panama, you found Honda, Nissan, Kia, Subaru, Mitsubishi, Ford, and Chevy, but no European cars). There were also very few full size or oversize vehicles, or large pick up trucks. I didn't see any Lincoln, Buick, Chrysler, Land Rover, Rolls Royce, Volvo, or SUV styles. Certainly there were no Hummers. Most streets in Rio were one way only. Mercedes Benz did have a big presence in passenger vans and armored trucks.

Mercedes Benz armored truck

Chapter Five

BANDA DE IPANEMA

Saturday, February 2, 2008

Today we slept in until around 11:30 am. Shari prepared for us a breakfast of toast, coffee, and fruit salad (succulent watermelon, red seedless grapes the size of unshelled walnuts and banana slices). Our goal for today was to catch the Ipanema Street Parade at 4:00 pm. This parade was widely recognized as a highlight fun event of the Carnaval season. Thus, it was one of the largest and most popular of the street parades.

We left the apartment around 3:15 pm, and walked towards Copacabana Beach. Avenida Atlantico runs the length of Copacabana Beach. Walking south on Avenida Atlantico would lead us to Ipanema Beach, since the two beaches were in proximity to each other.

Copacabana Beach

Copacabana Beach

Along the paved part of the sidewalk of Avenida Atlantico, vendors were selling jewelry, towels, shirts, dresses, refrigerator magnets, key chains, wall ornaments, beach wraps, and food concessions such as skewered BBQ'd meats, corn on the cob, beer, soda, bottled water, etc.

Although it was hot and muggy, Copacabana Beach was not as crowded as I had expected. I was extremely surprised to see that many people on the beach, both men and women, were overweight; maybe they were tourists. I had fully expected to see only lean, trim, beautiful bodies; but everywhere I looked I saw bulging stomachs, loose skin hanging over the sides of the swim suits, and big butts. There was no need for me to feel embarrassed about being overweight in this crowd! I would fit right in with everyone. Some people are very dark tanned, while others with white skin were bright pink. I winced looking at the flaming pink skin – these people were in for some serious suffering in a couple of hours with their second and third degree sunburns turning darker red by the moment.

In the heat and humidity we walked along the sunny side of Avenida Atlantico, just feeling hotter and hotter. Finally, we realized that it would be cooler walking on the other side of the street, which was shaded with trees, as were the side streets. We detoured from the beach and used, instead, residential streets, with their shaded canopies of overhanging trees along the lengths of the streets. The relief of walking in the cooler shade of the trees was immediately noticeable!

The homes and apartment entrances in the residential areas were all well maintained and clean, with perfectly groomed yards and gardens. Every residence was set apart from its neighbor with decorative painted iron bars that enhance the appearance of each individual "kingdom."

Just about every sidewalk had a kaleidoscope pattern of cut pieces of color tile set into concrete. Wherever you walked, the sidewalks were tiled and colorful.

All the tile pieces were handset, but unfortunately few areas were completely level. This was meaningful, because when it rained, as it did often, the water collected in unexpected puddles into which unwary pedestrians stepped, getting their shoes and feet wet. The patterns also allowed small particles of trash to collect inside the ridges of the tile sides. From my apartment window I have watched shopkeepers across the street endlessly sweep the same area in front of their shops over and over again, constantly uprooting new particles of trash lodged in the tile that were missed just a few broom strokes earlier.

TIP: Be courteous. Please don't litter.

As much noise and traffic as there was throughout the night and day, there was not a noticeable sound of sirens, such as those of police cars or emergency vehicles. In fact, with the hundreds of thousands of visitors to the city during Carnaval, there was not a noticeably heavy police presence. I noticed a few armed policemen, usually in the middle of the street directing traffic or on a congested corner, but I did not notice any marked patrol cars circling around, or armed soldiers with AK 47's on the street, which was a common sight in some other countries.

I did notice that every building, every store, and every restaurant had its own set of "private eyes" watching every customer. These private eyes were usually dressed like the customers, and normally stand near the entrances of the business (or building). Their job was not to greet. It was very clear they were there to discourage shoplifting, or vagrancy, or people snooping. They were all ages, men and women, young girls and young boys. It reminded me of going into some private businesses in California, where even the little children wandered through the aisles to keep an eye on you and what you were doing. In one business, there were men in suits with wireless transmitters commenting to each other regarding people entering and/or leaving. They followed "suspicious characters" until satisfied that the suspect was legit. But even if the customer was determined to be legit, that didn't stop the eye-balling during the remainder of their shopping. Sometimes in the stores the private eyes outnumbered the customers.

Finally, we reached the start point for the Banda de Ipanema parade. Because this parade was widely publicized as a highlight fun event of the Carnaval season, it resulted in huge crowds that gathered to participate. For the most part, other street parades, also known as "blocos," were not completely organized events. For them, vehicles with loudspeakers materialized out of nowhere. They began by blaring samba music as they slowly drove down a street. Hearing the music, people dropped what they were doing and joined in behind the vehicle, singing, dancing, and drinking. There was no official start or end point for these parades. People joined in for as long as they had time or energy, or, until the music stopped.

The gathering time for the Banda de Ipanema parade was rumored to be at 4:00 pm; we arrived at the gathering spot at 4:15 pm. Mike wasn't worried too much about being late; he had the feeling we could catch up with the rest of the parade if it had already started. It finally started at 5:30 pm. Meanwhile, the adjoining streets and sidewalks, which were blocked from vehicular traffic, had become more dense with people. When we first arrived, there was a lot of room to move around and turn to do things. But as greater numbers of people gathered, the space became tighter and tighter.

Finally the space was so tight that you couldn't move without elbowing someone else. And still the crowd became more condensed. The crowd was standing together like tall blades of grass, just waiting for the parade to start. Through the mass of people, vendors were inching along around people, and through the middle of groups, selling water, beer, shots of whiskey or fermented sugar cane, confetti, party head bands, t shirts, jewelry, and flashy items.

There were also non parade participants collecting aluminum cans. Throughout the trip, I noticed that only aluminum cans seemed to have a value, not plastic or glass. It was noticeable that many people were out collecting cans, not just one person here or there. On one occasion, I saw a woman reaching into a trash container on the street, lifting out an aluminum can and squashing it under her foot; but she left it there on the ground. Several people came by with their collection bags looking into the same trash container for aluminum cans, but missing the one already squashed left on the ground; they would leave without finding any. Finally, a child came by, saw the can on the ground, picked it up, and added it to the collection in her bag.

Standing in a tight crowd of people waiting for the parade to start, I thought I detected an attempt to pickpocket me. I felt three fingers move along my back. Then the sensation ended. It could have been anyone – people standing behind me, people moving past me, or people trying to regain their balance.

TIP: Beware of unknown people crowding you. Pickpockets come in all sizes, shapes and ages. Check for your belongings inconspicuously; otherwise, you are showing pickpockets where you have your valuables.

But I wasn't worried. I had my passport, money, and picture ID in a passport wallet in my front pocket on one side with its strap securely tied to my belt. On the other front pocket I had my pocket size camera strapped securely to my belt. I carried my backpack on my shoulders, which sometimes knocked people behind me off balance when I would turn to see something. One concerned person told me that I needed to be careful because the backpack could easily be opened from the back, and the contents stolen.

I didn't really have anything of value stored in the backpack. All I was carrying in the backpack throughout most of the trip were extra clothes, a sweater, an umbrella, my medications, and my sunglasses. As the crowd continued to visibly increase in size and density, greater numbers of people arrived dressed in costumes, whether it be a partial costume of a head band, a hat or a mask, or a full body costume. Any costume was a good costume. It could be a plain "cat-in-the-hat" head covering, a New Year's Eve style hat, costume ball clothing, superhero clothing, even a USC Trojan football outfit complete with logo. There were dancers on stilts, bare-chested cowboys, and people (men and women) dressed as nuns in miniskirts. There were obvious drag queens that weren't at all pretty (maybe because they weren't trying to be pretty). The only type of costume that was rare to see was that of a furry animal, probably because it would be too hot and heavy to wear. The costumes were intended to make the parade more colorful and festive. It was an intoxicating atmosphere of sight and sound.

While waiting for the parade to start, individuals, and/or groups of people in various areas of the street, would just start singing, beating makeshift drums, and dancing, while those surrounding them would join in and do the same, singing and dancing in place. The crowd consisted of everything from babies in strollers, to children with their parents, to groups of teens, to couples, to senior citizens. There were obvious families gathered, with groups of relatives, school groups, international groups, sports teams, singles, and people who seemed to know each other from somewhere else. It was like attending one big family reunion.

Finally, the loudspeakers of the truck intended to start leading the parade came to life blaring with Samba music. The crowd inched forward a little, then a little more, until it was moving at a steady slow pace down the street.

While the music being played was "samba," the crowd dance moves were whatever matched the music beat! Samba, as taught in dance schools, just does not work while dancing in a street parade. The rhythm and dance movements are more free form, while still matching the beat of the music.

In the oppressive heat and humidity, the crowd danced behind the Piped Piper truck down Ipanema Beach, then turning down a large boulevard that had been blocked to traffic. The size of the crowd had grown considerably larger than football arena game size; it was thousands of people now participating. While this is a highlighted "official" street parade, it was just a reflection of other smaller street parades ("blocos, or pick-up" parades) also taking place throughout the city at various times of the day and night for the five day celebration of Carnaval.

Almost as important as the music truck, the beer truck distributing free beer

We danced with the crowd behind the truck with its blaring music until about 7:30 pm. It's a blur to my memory if we danced all the way to the end of the parade, or just dropped out at some point because we were hungry and tired. All throughout the parade route people would join in out of nowhere, and drop out, at any point. The purpose of the street parade was to dance with the parade for as long as you wanted, to join in the festivity of Carnaval.

We were hungry, tired, damp with sweat, and overheated. We would dance in the crowd for about half an hour, stop, join back in with the dance crowd again for a period of time, stop for a breather, and so on. Sometimes our stops were to do "window shopping" of the vendors along the parade route.

Each vendor we encountered would eye us suspiciously at first, like they were just waiting to pounce on us for supposedly shoplifting their items displayed for sale. But after seeing us interested in buying many items at a time,they would bend over backwards to show us their wares. Ah, it must have been a blow to that Irish in Mike, who steadfastly refused to flash the power of the color green (e.g. US currency); rather, he would make every effort to use Brazilian currency, in color denominations of blue ($2), pink ($5), brownish pink ($10), yellow ($20) and light tan ($50).

Finally, we had enough of vendor shopping and of street dancing. We set off to find a restaurant ("Gula Gula") recommended in the tourist guide. We walked up and down numerous city blocks, looking for this particular restaurant, thinking we were on the wrong street or in the wrong area of the city. Finally, we determined that the Gula Gula restaurant we were looking for had either been torn down or replaced by an apartment building. This is one of several instances when we would be looking for a particular business as mentioned in the guide book, but finding it had been replaced by something else, or no longer existed.

We had passed several beer cafes — small beer shops with three or four tables outside of the building on the sidewalk where people were sitting, eating snack foods, and enjoying their beer. But this was not what we wanted. We needed solid dinner food. We kept looking for a cafe or restaurant. Shari finally decided we should stop at a place we had already passed twice. It looked like a fancy beer shop to me but Shari was certain that they would have good food to eat. When we passed it previously she asked a young man in a suit standing outside, who appeared to be a maitre d', if they served "comida" (e.g., food). He nodded politely and said, "sim" (e.g., yes). It was named, "De Vassa." We decided to return to it, and went in. And thus began the third memorable meal of the trip.

De Vassa turned out to be the restaurant for a major brewery of the same name in Brazil. At this location, they served everything from steak, seafood, pasta, sandwiches, desserts, to a full bar featuring hard liquors and the brand name beer "De Vassa" in four types—pilsner, medium red, dark, and "India" (e.g., very strong).

Mike ordered "feijoada," a mixture of various meats (today it included pork ribs, beef, and sausage) in a black bean sauce. Shari ordered, "Maria Bonita," a type of corned beef cooked with strips of onion and thick large fries that were crunchy on the outside, but hearty in texture and tasty to eat. I ordered "Frengo (something, something),"

48

which turned out to be thinly sliced chicken stuffed with mushrooms and covered in a creamy sauce.

By this time we had all come to an informal agreement that "your food is my food," and vice versa. Throughout the meal, we would pass portions back and forth from plate to plate. We were like fish in an aquarium tank when the feeding takes place – a nibble here, a nibble there, a gulp, another gulp, float stationary for a few moments, then dart in for the next nibble. For my drink I pointed to a menu item indicating a large pitcher of beer. But the waiter shook his head, indicating with his hands that the pitcher was maybe "too large for one person." To me the size as indicated on the photo in the menu looked to be about six large glasses of brew, but I was in no position to argue my case with the waiter since he spoke neither English nor Spanish. I pointed to the pint glass size.

When my beer came, I gulped it down, then quickly motioned to the waiter to bring another. I did the same with that, and again motioned to the waiter to bring another (it was hot outside, I was thirsty, and the beer flowed smoothly down my throat). After I downed the third beer, the waiter's eyes grew large as I ordered another; I believe he was re-evaluating my beer capacity. But when the fourth beer came, the food also came at the same time. With the various shared meals, I grew full quickly, and my thirst was quenched.

Meanwhile, Mike ordered his traditional "café con leche" (e.g., expresso with hot milk. The expresso comes in tiny little cups, while the hot milk is served in teapots). On the prior day on the cable car at Sugarloaf, a woman told Shari of the national Brazilian drink called "Caipirinha" (fermented sugar cane with lemon and ice, very similar to a margarita). Shari ordered a Caipirinha. The saying is"One Caipirinha, you feel good. Two Caipirinhas you are speaking Portuguese fluently. Three, everyone is your friend. Four, you feel that you are flying. Five, you are wondering, "Who am I, and, who are you?"

Shari stopped at one Caipirinha. She felt good, and still knew who we were! After dinner, we were so full we decided to take the bus back to the apartment. It turned out to be a wise choice. Walking in the parade and then looking around for a place to eat had taken us a lot further in distance than we realized. The bottoms of my feet were swollen, the sides of my individual toes had grown blisters, my calves hurt to stand up, my knees were creaking, and any movement caused pain in my upper hips.

TIP: Always wear comfortable walking shoes.

When we returned to the apartment, Shari immediately headed for the shower. As dead tired as we were from the street parade, it didn't stop Mike from his imitation of what a strutting Mick Jagger would look like if he were dancing the Samba. Mike's dance moves were still hot! Finally, we all hit the sack, thinking we would be out cold in a few moments. But there would only be intermittent sleep for us. The impromptu street parades with drums banging, the noise from the cars and buses, the honking of car horns, and the singing and shouting of people out on the street even into the early morning hours would keep us from peaceful slumber throughout the night.

Chapter Six

GREGORIAN HIGH MASS

Sunday February 3, 2008

The next morning, it did not dawn. Instead, we were greeted with dark black clouds in the sky and a downpour of heavy rain. It had started raining in the early morning hours around 3:00 am, dampening the party spirit and enthusiasm of the revelers on the street; but that also resulted in lengthening the time we could peacefully sleep. This was the morning of our planned visit to the "Gregorian High Mass" at San Bento Monastery Chapel, the local Benedictine monastery. It was an event that Shari and Mike had carefully planned for in the months preceding our trip. Mike and Shari were very excited to be attending this special Sunday service. I had no interest at all in attending it.

On a previous trip to Austria, Shari and Mike had attended a Gregorian High Mass in Vienna, and were so enthralled by the music of approximately one hundred fifty choir members chanting the music of Hayden's Nelson mass, accompanied by a full orchestra with four professional soloists. So they expected something similar here because according to the Brazilian travel guide:

"To get to the monastery you pass through the awesomely wide and frantically busy Avenida Presidente Vargas, and another impressive street, the Igreja da Candelaria and Rue Visconde de Inhauma, which is (Brazilian) Navy territory (attached to a naval base located in Rio). At the street level is an elevator to take you up five stories to the chapel. The elevator delivers you to a beautiful setting, surrounded by trees and singing birds to the secluded workplace of the Benedictine monks who live in cloister here. The chapel is famous for its sung masses in the rich Gregorian tradition, which are particularly uplifting. Inside the ornate and grandiose interior, one is struck by the intricacy of the woodcarving and amount of gold leaf that has been applied to the interior of the chapel."

To Shari and Mike, this was a must see, and must experience, in Rio! If I had also read the travel guide ahead of time, I would probably have been eager to attend this event too.

But I hadn't read the travel guide, and I was not all that enthused about going to a Gregorian High Mass. To me, it meant a long, drawn out Sunday service in Latin that would last between two to three hours. Before the trip started, when discussing points of interest, I had told them I did not want to attend this event. But I didn't make a major issue out of it, thinking that something else would come up, and we would pass on it. But here it was, Sunday morning. Shari and Mike were preparing to go, even though it was pouring rain outside; earlier in the morning there had even been thunder and bolts of lightning. With the expectation of a two to three hour service, I protested, "Why don't we just skip it and instead go to a local quickie Sunday mass that will only last an hour?" But they would not hear of it. It had to be the Gregorian High Mass today! Finally I told them, as my trump card, "If I catch pneumonia going out in this rain, there will be hell to pay!" Of course, it went without saying that I already had pneumonia, and that I had it before I even started the trip to Rio. So it was an empty threat.

San Bento Monastery Chapel

Off we traipsed into the rain, stepping into the puddles hidden in the uneven sidewalks, getting our shoes and feet wet. We walked about eight blocks to the subway, then about fourteen smaller blocks from the subway to the monastery. When we arrived at the supposed address of the monastery, dripping wet from the rain and humidity, we found only one long concrete wall about ten feet high. We followed the wall, looking for the elevator to take us up the hill, but only found a driveway leading up the hill. We walked up the driveway the equivalent of five stories high, in the rain, and found the monastery at the end of the driveway. The monastery was built between 1617 and 1641. It was truly beautiful inside.

We arrived just as the Sunday mass was starting. What a delightful experience of getting up early, braving the rain and the puddles, and the long walk up the hill. Alas, today there would be no uplifting sung mass "in the rich Gregorian tradition." There was no orchestra, no one hundred and fifty member choir, and no best to sing in unison. They looked to be in their late thirties, as they chanted in Portuguese every reading, response, and acclamation of the mass. Maybe the normal size of the group of monks was larger, but on this day it sounded like we only had "monk leftovers." The poor monks didn't even sound half- hearted in their singing; they sounded more like they were barely awake at 10:00 am. Their harmony was far from melodious. It sounded like every one of them was struggling to blend their voices into a melody while trailing each other in their words and tempo. The monks must have run low on wine supplies the previous day, because their Gregorian was not "high" enough. Shari felt bad for them, and even suggested that I join in to help them sing since I am familiar with Latin, and with singing Latin mass parts. But they weren't singing in Latin. They were singing in Portuguese. It was a Portuguese Gregorian style High Mass.

There were some pluses though to this service......the homily, which we did not understand, was in Portuguese. It was only ten minutes long, not the thirty to forty five minutes I expected. The mass service lasted only a little over an hour. The biggest plus – there was no Sunday collection taken. For once I had my meager donation ready in my pocket to put into the basket. Now I had extra cash to spend instead on beer!

The small chapel had about two hundred and fifty people crowded into it for the mass. The sides of the chapel were constructed of dark oak sculpted in a Baroque style with gilded sides detailing the outlines of the wood carvingssoloists. Instead, it was the feeble voices of the four young monks trying their.

At head level between the arches were wooden sculptures all in the same design of the same bishop with the same crosier (staff) of a two tier cross. About ten feet above the bishops were sculptures all of the same design of the same pope, with his crosier of a three tier cross. You could differentiate between the bishops and the pope by the tiers of their crosiers, and their miters (the pointed hats). Between the statues of the bishops/pope were smaller arches fanning out around various individual ceramic sculptures of saints surrounded by cherubs. I only recognized the sculpture of St. Anthony of Padua.

The seating inside the chapel consisted of long wooden benches that swayed uneasily as if the bolts in the joints were loose, and would collapse at any moment from the additional weight of just one more mass participant. There were only rear seats available when we arrived. The altar was obscured behind a large pillar in front of these seats. Nonetheless, Shari and I took these seats, while Mike remained standing at the side aisle. About ten minutes passed, with Shari straining to see around the pillar down the main aisle. She suggested generously and sweetly, "Pancho, let's change seats so you can see what's happening." I responded, "Nah, that's all right. I know from experience what is happening and what it looks like." Anyway, there was nothing to see. The original altar was covered in a sheer cloth because the chapel was undergoing renovation. While some details of the altar sculptures and design were visible, at this time the overall impact of the beautiful original architecture could only be imagined.

Walking back to the subway after mass, although they didn't say it, I think Shari and Mike were grateful to hear only my limited sarcastic comments, or commentary, regarding the uplifting experience of the high mass.

As we crossed a street, we noticed on one of the main boulevards that floats were being prepared and staged for the Sambadrome competition starting later that night; the competition is spread over two nights. Because of the rain, the floats were covered with tarps, with no one actively working on them. This was an advantage to us because it allowed us to get up close to see the floats without impeding people or the work being done on them.

Floats being staged for Sambadrome competition

We returned to the apartment as drowned rats. Shari immediately suggested that I take a hot shower to regain my body temperature. Then we rested for several hours, with them overhearing, I think, my continued limited sarcastic commentary to myself in my room about the uplifting Gregorian High mass experience.

After several hours, the rain finally stopped completely. We ventured out to find a place to have lunch/dinner, and to find another restaurant recommended in the travel guide. It was supposed to be located only a few blocks away, at the side of the beach, but it was nowhere to be found. We went back and forth several times, checking the addresses, but where it should have been there was now another restaurant in its place. We finally decided to try out this restaurant instead. Later, after we were seated, we noticed a sign inside the restaurant referencing the original restaurant we were seeking. This restaurant had absorbed, or replaced, the original one. We had another excellent meal, but one with a twist. Mike ordered the steak Oswaldo, Shari a sausage pizza, and I requested the breaded filet of Holstein. I figured that a "Holstein" could only mean red meat.

The meals were delicious, but from the beginning of the meal I could taste a hint of something fishy. Finally, I turned over with my fork something that looked like a strip of caramelized onion on top of the meat. As soon as I saw the silvery backing, I knew immediately that it was fish related! It was a sliver of anchovy, one of four on top of my Holstein. The taste of the anchovy was making my stomach turn. I get an allergic reaction when I taste or eat fish; I get nauseous, my throat constricts, and I gag. I can be eating something and immediately know that it contains fish because of these bodily reactions. I don't get the same reactions, though, from eating shrimp, crab, or lobster. Lately, I have tried octopus. I found that I can stomach it if there is enough beer to drown out the chewy texture.

Meanwhile, the taste of the anchovy had permeated my meat. As he had so generously done on many other occasions, Mike offered to switch meals with me; I took him up on his offer. Unfortunately, while switching the meal, one little piece of carrot was left on my plate sitting there all by itself looking lonely. I speared it with my fork, and popped it into my mouth. This little piece must have been sitting in a puddle of anchovy juice, because as I swallowed it, I began choking, like something was stuck in my throat. Shari and Mike immediately responded to see if I needed the Heimlich maneuver performed on me, but I was able to nod my head "no." That was it for my meal. I had lost all desire to finish eating my dinner.

After our dinner, we returned to the apartment for more rest. About two hours later we heard a loud noise, like that of a speaker attached to a car making announcements as it travels down the street; only instead of announcements it was the sound of music. It was a street parade coming right down our street. Mike was still tired; he just wanted to lean out of the apartment window to watch the parade go by. Shari and I went downstairs to watch the parade up close. We ended up joining in with the crowd passing by.

A "bloco" approaching

We danced in the parade with hundreds of other people down the main street, closed off now to traffic. We danced down to the beach, then down Avenida Atlantica.

Finally, we grew tired of dancing. We stepped up onto the sidewalk, letting the parade continue on, and leaving us behind. By total coincidence, we had stopped at a beach street fair. Instead of returning immediately to the apartment, we walked through the aisles of the street fair looking at clothing, jewelry, magnets, key chains, sandalwear, sculptured masks, etc. We left some vendors very content and happy after we left their booths with our purchases. Finally, we ran out of cash; we had been careful all through the trip not to carry all our money on us at one time. We returned to the apartment with our purchases, and found that Mike was not there. He decided to join in with the parade long after we left, and was too far behind us to catch up to us. By now it was about 11:00 pm., so we turned in.

Incidentally, my pneumonia, which had been improving up to Sunday, started into a relapse. It must have been from the downpour of rain on the way to that stimulating Gregorian High Mass.

Chapter Seven

SAMBADROME

Another night of revelry noise on the street had kept Shari awake throughout the night. She had tried using earplugs (and even given me a pair to use), but they weren't working for either of us to keep out the noise. Mike and I had found other ways to sleep through most of the noises. But tonight the sounds must have been louder than before. I woke up around 3:30 am and looked out the window at a disturbance on the street. There appeared to be a young man lying on his back on the sidewalk across the street in front of a shop. Another young man was next to him, poking and prodding him, yelling at him, and trying to get him to respond to get up. But he remained lying there without movement. Finally, his friend left him there and went somewhere.

A short while later, when I looked out the window again, the man lying on the street was now covered with a blanket. As I watched, a group of people, singing and laughing loudly, and walking up the same side of the street, approached him from one direction, while a man on a bicycle was coming down the street towards him from the other direction. The man on the bicycle moved closer to the buildings to avoid hitting the group coming towards him. Unfortunately, he did not immediately see the man lying on the ground. It looked like the bicycle ran over the man, but the man didn't even flinch. Several hours later, when I looked out again, there was no longer a body lying out there.

Shari got up around 10:30 am, and, as she had done on the previous mornings, made a breakfast of toast, coffee, and fruit salad (watermelon, large walnut sized grapes, and banana) for her and for us. It was another day of rain – light rain at times, heavy rain at other times, with sprinkles in between. Shari ventured out alone to do some grocery shopping.

It became for us a needed day of rest, since the evening would be devoted to the Sambadrome, which would live up to being the highlight of the trip for us.

After flittering away most of the day, we started out around 5:45 pm towards the area in Ipanema where a tour bus would pick us up to take us directly to the Sambadrome stadium (a specially constructed arena used only for the Samba competitions at annual Carnaval).

When Mike had been making the arrangements to rent the apartment from the owner ("Debbie," who used to live in Rio but now lived in New York City), he mentioned our intention to buy tickets for the Sambadrome. Debbie suggested that we allow Lamborghini to buy the tickets for us since he was already familiar with the process, and also any particulars that would be unknown to us. Then we wouldn't have to hassle trying to get the tickets at the last minute, and we could get the best seats available for what we were willing to pay. We took her advice.

TIP: Use services of concierge, or similar person, whenever possible.

Carnaval, the major annual event of Rio, refers to a season of festivity lasting five days. The Sambadrome competition is the highlight, and culmination of Carnaval. Samba is the music and heart of Brazil. The Samba competition took place over a two night period, with six Samba schools competing one night, and the other six schools the next night. The Samba competition (a.k.a., the marching of the schools) was scheduled both days to start at 10:00 pm, and end around 5:00 am the next morning. Whichever school won the competition had official, recognized, bragging rights for the whole year of being the school that best exemplified the music and heart of Brazil.

Even though the guide book suggested arrival at the stadium around 10:00 pm when the crowd was warming up, we planned on arriving at 9:00 pm to get good seats. We caught the tour bus, which was making continuous runs to/from the Sambadrome, at about 8:30 pm.

The bus arrived at the Sambadrome close to 9:00 pm. We were disappointed to find that our "reserve seating" was not for individual seats, but for the concrete stands of "Sector 7," the mid-section of the stadium (from ground level to the top). The stands were already close to eighty five percent full. We could only find space at the highest level of the section, which is about six stories high from the parade course level. It still was an excellent spot to view the competition of the schools when they were making their approach, and as they passed in front of us. Later we were told that Sector 7 was actually the best general public viewing section, and across from the judges box.

Each school had about an hour within which to complete its presentation. The twelve main schools take the competition for the title each year very seriously. If there was a particular school you wanted to see or support, you needed to buy your ticket for the night they were performing. The reputed six best schools, as determined from the previous year's competition, always competed on the second night of the competition. Our tickets were for this second night!

Just like any sporting event here in the USA, there was grandstand seating, box seats, reserve, and general admission. As constructed, the Sambadrome had one side with general admission, and reserve seating; the opposite side had grandstand seating, and the entire midsection of that side with built-in box seating, the prime viewing area for the parade.

The box section was three levels high, with what appeared to be fifteen sections of box seats. Each box section had twelve seats. I could see from my position on the opposite side that there was an average of thirty five to forty people crammed inside each section except for the judge's box.

I could also see inside each box section a white shirt, black bow tie waiter serving food and drinks. Because they were so overcrowded, many of the box sections had people straddling the concrete railing of the box to get a better view (or maybe have "a seat"). Although it could have easily happened, I did not see anyone fall from the railing. I overhead a man next to me telling his friends that if he would have known the box sections only cost fifty thousand Brazilian Reales (approximately thirty thousand dollars US), he would have paid for a box section instead of the reserve seats he was in on our side.

In essence, there were no seats in the stadium except for the few in the box section. The remainder of the "seating" in the stadium on both sides consisted of concrete steps. Foam seating pads were being distributed, but Shari and Mike had brought with us fancy foam seats that had a backing which allowed us to be able to recline. But it didn't matter. The only time we would find to sit would be in the short time between school presentations, a time period of about fifteen minutes to half an hour. If a person were sitting, they would not be able to see over the crowd standing in front of them to the parade route below. However, during the break in schools, we could sit, and rest our feet, on the concrete steps in front of us. As we would find throughout the night, this set up was a welcome relief when it occurred.

The Sambadrome competition is a huge parade that travels down a straight course equivalent to about seven football fields in length. Picture the chariot race of the movie, Ben Hur, or the Rose Bowl, as a straight course rather than being circular, and you are looking at the Sambadrome.

It is a spectacle that incorporates elements of New York's Times Square New Year's Eve celebration, Macy's Thanksgiving Day Parade, the night atmosphere of Las Vegas, Mardi Gras in New Orleans, the Rose Parade, Oktoberfest celebrations, and the typical neighborhood Halloween trick-or-treating all rolled into a competition between the Samba Schools.

The public announcer made sure that as each school started its competition it had a rousing introduction. He sounded like an announcer at a professional wrestling match but, of course, announcing in Portuguese. After about five minutes of lively introduction, a major fireworks show would erupt.

How can I describe the fireworks show preceding each school, except to say that for each school it was the equivalent of a huge Fourth of July fireworks display here in the USA. Flashy, flowery fireworks would burst for about ten minutes, followed by about five to ten minutes of the type of fireworks that look and sound like the burst of cannon fire. These bursts were so rapid and intense that they could be compared easily to witnessing a major battle engagement of two fleets on the high seas. I have seen in our local newspaper back home that every year the City Council had to authorize funds of about twenty thousand dollars for the annual Fourth of July fireworks display for a medium size show. The fireworks preceding each school here in the Sambadrome easily exceeded the fireworks shows I was accustomed to seeing back home.

At the conclusion of the fireworks, only then could the each school in the competition start its march down the parade course.

Meanwhile, what I believed was a police helicopter hovered over the stadium the whole evening with "flashing spotlights" to keep aerial spectators away.

Each year it is customary that each school selected its own theme. Within their presentation towards winning the competition, each school could construct from eight to twelve elaborate floats to illustrate the school theme.

Just as each float in the Rose Parade needed to conform its theme to the overall theme of the Rose Parade, in the Samba competitions each school must conform their floats to the main school theme of the Carnaval year. The selection of the individual float themes was "anything goes" as long as it met the school theme for the year. The two night Samba competition (parade), which features thousands of scantily clad and elaborately plumed dancers, was the high point of the Carnaval celebration. It was televised nationally in a country with an estimated one hundred eighty five million people, and televised internationally.

This year there was only one float theme which caused consternation when it was proposed. The float, designed by Viradouro, a top rated Rio Samba school, was to be a simulation of the Holocaust, with emancipated corpses and a dancing Hitler. It was intended to remind Carnaval attendees of past horrors to humanity, and to prevent their re-occurrence by "giving goose-bumps." However, the float was barred from being constructed after the Rio state court stepped in. The Jewish Federation of Rio de Janeiro had sued under Brazilian federal laws to prohibit Nazi propaganda and racism in Brazil.

After the fireworks, sections of costumed dancers began their march down the parade course. The sections were led first by "bahias" (older women who are the matrons of the school). Leading the bahias were small groups of choreographed dancers performing precision dancing. The sections were about fifteen people wide, and consisted of twenty, thirty, or forty rows of dancers, all dressed in their dazzling costumes of the same pattern and color, each costume handmade to be identical to the others within the same group.

Bahias leading a school

Each school was led by "a Las Vegas style show girl" dressed in an elaborate one-of-a- kind costume.

Showgirl on the head of the Peacock Float. Dark specks on float body were human dancers who came alive to dance

Within in each section all the participants dressed alike in the same colors and designs; they differed in color and design from the section preceding it, and the one following it. The costumes were dazzling arrays of color, reflective materials, and detail. As examples, there were sections of people dressed as types of flowers, dolphins, lobsters being cooked in their individual pots, conquistadores, miniature boats and cars, French revolutionaries, natives in huts, a platoon of Napoleonic soldiers, skeletons, insects, butterflies, bees, spiders, and many other characterizations. With section after section of dancers, it looked like armies marching in precision down the course; all dressed alike within their section, but looking differently from the dancers before them, and after them. This resulted in a blinding sea of color and spectacle.

(Additional floats and dancers page 133)

Floats seemed to be interspersed after every four sections of dancers. Most of the floats were illuminated from within, and all the floats seemed to have been built with animated parts. Major parts of each float that appeared from a distance to be decoration only later came alive as dancers exited what previously appeared to be inanimate material. People were disguised and hidden on each float as part of the background, and, after coming alive to dance for a few moments, would return to a stationary pose to again appear inanimate. Doors would pop open, people come out and dance, then retreat back into their disguised spot. Any part of a float that was turning or spinning had a human person inside of it, sometimes providing the propulsion for the part, which could be a sphere, a carousel, etc.

In the middle of each school's presentation, live singers with wireless microphones accompanied the school's sound amplifying truck singing the school song selected for the year, over and over again, the whole length of the parade course. The sound was transmitted from the truck to hundreds of speakers lining the parade route (just above the box sections), so that the whole stadium was enveloped in the same music at the same time at the same pitch.

School's music truck (white vehicle far right)

Immediately preceding the live singers, a percussion section of an estimated three hundred to four hundred players/dancers marched, with approximately ten drum majors dressed in colors similar to their section so that they blended in with their group. They kept their subsections, within the overall section, in rhythm and beat to the music.

Before each school could start its portion of the competition, the parade route had to be completely clear of the preceding school's participants, trash and debris. This meant the previous school had to completely have exited the parade course before the next school could start. As we would see for ourselves, the final float of each school would shoot out glittering confetti into the air. Behind the last float the "pooper scoopers" would be walking, sweeping up the trash, confetti, and debris (things that had fallen off the dancers/marchers, or the floats themselves). There weren't any live animals in the parade so there was no "animal poop" to pick up (as there is in a regular parade with live animals in it). As the "pooper scoopers" filled up their plastic trash containers, they would empty the containers into a trash truck also following the last float.

A highlight expected of the "pooper scoopers" was that at least one member of the cleanup detail would perform fancy Samba footwork and dancing for the entertainment of the audience while they were cleaning up. Once the "pooper scoopers" reached the end of the parade course, and exited it, then the course was considered ready for the next school presentation. It is during the "pooper scooper show" when people could sit and rest, but then they would miss seeing the show!

As midnight approached I began to experience another relapse of my pneumonia symptoms. My body felt feverish, I had coughing spasms, and a pounding headache. Since the Sambadrome competition was the highlight of the trip, and the single most costly item after the cost of the flight and the apartment rental, I wasn't about to let this opportunity pass. Shari and Mike offered to cut short the evening if I needed to return to the apartment to rest. However, I was determined to do everything I could to last through at least three schools (e.g., until around 1:00 am).

As the night progressed, soon it was four schools, then five schools; finally we were down to the last school. I found myself drawn into the beat of the music, and dancing to the music throughout the whole night. It has been a good twenty years since I have danced to more than a couple of songs at one sitting. It seemed over the years that my joints had hardened, and, after a few minutes of dancing, I needed to sit down to rest. Here, this music and the enthusiasm of the crowd permeated my bones. The dancing actually relieved the soreness of my feet from standing, and the effects of the pneumonia were felt less and less as the night progressed. By the time the last school ended around 5:00 am, only then did I feel the overall tiredness and the effect of being physically in another dimension.

While the Sambadrome competition was exciting, and the highlight of the trip, there were other aspects associated with this evening that helped make it memorable. Those other aspects were the people we met, and interacted with, during the evening. On the tour bus, there were two pretty Latina sisters (not nuns, but from the same family) named Judith and Erica. Sitting on the bus seats in front of us, they looked to be the same size. But when they stood up, Judith was shorter than me, while Erica was taller than me. "We share everything but our boyfriends," they giggled. They were from Modesto, CA (Mike said they lived about four blocks away from where his sister lives). Judith was twenty eight, while Erica was twenty six. Judith had spent one and half years as an exchange student at the Universidad da Rio de Janeiro, in Rio. She still had friends living in the Leblon area (ahem, the "upper crust") of the city. She and Erica were staying with those people. They had befriended "Dora," a lady in her sixties traveling by herself from Sydney, Australia. There were the two young men in front of us, dressed as Batman and Robin, from Waikiki, Hawaii.

They were very friendly, and easy to talk to. I tried to tell them that it was proper hospitality for them to invite us to visit them in Hawaii using a Spanish phrase, "Mi casa es tu casa" (e.g., "my house is your house"). Apparently, they already knew what it meant because they didn't invite us to Hawaii to stay in their home. There was a "young looking" mother in her late thirties with her two teenage daughters. Although she appeared young to me, having teenage daughters she couldn't have been that young. She was so excited to be there watching this competition; meanwhile, the daughters were bored to death. Her husband/ boyfriend kept falling asleep the whole night. There were two girls from India in front of us; they were students from London who made this trip just to experience Carnaval. There was a lady about sixty five years old from Indonesia, who spoke very good English. And last, but not least, there was Carlos.

Carlos was sixty years old, from São Paulo, Brazil. He overheard Mike saying something in Portuguese. From that moment on, for the rest of the evening, Carlos was Mike's best friend. They were inseparable (at least from Carlos' point of view). He kept buying Mike beer (Shari and I were standing next to Mike and we weren't offered beer), explaining the nuances of the various schools to Mike, telling him all that Brazil has to offer, even splitting his chicken dinner with Mike. A couple of times I glanced backwards to watch Mike performing his Samba dancing next to the top retainer wall just behind us where there was room and space to breathe. Carlos was right there next to him dancing along as well, keeping him company. Mike didn't seem to mind his companionship.

Actually, Mike seemed to have the same effect on all the Brazilian people we encountered.

They were astounded that Mike, a tall, white man, could communicate with them, and that he had a decent command and pronunciation of the language. Shari and I kept struggling to communicate in Spanish, which a lot of Brazilians didn't understand. In fact, I had the hardest time trying to pronounce "Thank you" in Portuguese. The word is "obrigado." I would say everything but that particular word/pronunciation. I would say "Ombigado," or "Omigado," or "obregado." I'm still not sure I can say it right. Finally, I just settled for using a word that sounded similar to its Italian equivalent, "Gratzi," which everyone seemed to understand.

To his credit, Mike was the most prepared of the three of us for this trip. Mike had studied, and retained, knowledge of common phrases, pronunciations, exchange rates of currency, bus routes, subway routes, event turntables, and event site locations. At one point he even corrected Lamborghini, our local "expert," on the details of how to get across town. We had five months to prepare for the trip. I could barely make heads or tails of the travel brochures before getting overwhelmed with the details. I had even fallen asleep watching a Samba training DVD. With his knowledge of the city, and his pronunciation of the language, Mike was rightly given every respect by the waiters, the bus drivers, the doormen, the taxi drivers, and the workers in the various shops and stores where we made purchases.

TIP: Make an effort to learn a little about the country you are visiting. You will be amazed at the courtesy received back from the locals.

Shari had her own area of contribution as well. I had asked her, and Mike, to tell me during this trip that if at any time they detected a noticeable downhill slide in my health, and that I didn't seem to notice it myself, to let me know and I would stay, or return to the apartment. Meanwhile, they could continue participating without me in whatever planned activity was taking place.

Shari took my request to heart. From that moment on, she was like the mother hen looking after her little chick. She, and Mike, would frequently inquire throughout the day how I was feeling. When walking, Shari would hold on to my backpack straps so that I "wouldn't get lost." She would prepare breakfast and coffee in the morning. She would make sure I was eating, and including vegetables in my meals.

She would remind me to use my inhaler when I would get into coughing spasms, and remind me to take my medications at the appropriate times. When we would return to the apartment soaked by rain or perspiration, she would be after me to take a hot shower and change into warm dry clothes. She was determined to get me back home to California in one piece, that not being inside a coffin. I am grateful to Shari for all her prodding and care for me throughout the trip.

After the Sambadrome competition ended, we ran to catch our tour bus for our return. We had been forewarned that the bus service would only run for half an hour after the competition. But with all the various tour buses lined up to pick up their designated passengers, with people in the crowd elbowing each other out of the way trying to board their particular bus, and a disorganized bus loading area, it was like trying to find a needle in a haystack in a free-for-all mad dash for a prize. Finally, towards the end of the bus line, Mike spotted an empty bus approaching that was displaying our number. Our bus did not stop there at the end of the line for us. It traveled slowly all the way to the front of the line of parked buses, with the three of us, and many others, walking behind it waiting for it to stop. Mike commented that he was impressed with how the traffic controllers stayed calm in directing the loading of the buses. They didn't yell or scream at people to follow instructions; rather, they quietly and respectfully got people to comply.

Chapter Eight

CHURRASCO

Tuesday, February 5, 2008

We arrived back in the apartment from the Sambadrome about 6:00 am. Shari immediately made a beeline to the shower. Mike, in that imitable style of his, kept humming and singing the school songs we had just heard in the competitions, while dancing by himself to the Samba music he was humming. It made me smile to see Mike, as tired as he was, so much into the Samba spirit long after the blaring music of the Sambadrome had ended.

We slept and/or rested until around 3:30 pm. We decided that this would be a good day to sample one of Brazil's best known secrets – the Churrasco style of dining. Churrascos have made a name for themselves because of their style of serving food. Large chunks of meat selections are brought out on skewers to the table. If you indicate you are interested in the particular entrée, a slice of that meat is cut off from the chunk on the skewer right in front of you at the table and put on your plate.

At this particular Churrasco, seventeen various cuts of meat, including beef, pork, lamb, chicken, and sausage, were being offered. The seventeen cuts of meat offered (in Portuguese) were Picanha, Fraldinha, Maminha, Filé Mignon com Queijo, Alcatra, Cupim, Chuleta ao Alho, Lagarto Recheado, Costela de Boi, Costela de Porco, Pernil de Cameiro, Lombinho Recheado, Picanha Suina, Linguiça, Coração, Peru com Bacon, and Coxa de Frango — see, I knew you would recognize all of them. Now you know why we would just point to something on the menu and hope for the best. No need to ask the waiter for an explanation which we would not understand anyway.

It is up to the customer to say "yes" or "no" to more meat, or to skip some of the meats offered. You could have as much as you wanted, as often as you wanted. Some of the meat selections melted in my mouth, such as the filè mignon (a staple at every restaurant), the slightly salty rump roast (simply delicious), the chicken and the lamb. Some of the selections were tough to chew. Overall, most of the meats were too good to pass up.

Every time you looked up from your plate, another waiter would be at your elbow asking if you wanted a cut of the meat he was carrying on his skewer. For us who did not speak Portuguese, we just looked at the meat. If it looked tasty, we nodded or said, "si," for a slice to be cut. If we indicated "no," the waiter simply moved on to the next table, asking the same question, then the next table, and so on.

"Just leave both of them, please!"

There were even skewers of hot buttered garlic French bread. In addition, there was a buffet area offering various salads, meats in gravy, whole fish, sushi, and Brazilian style lasagna (pasta rolled over a loose gravy meat).

There was just no way we could leave the table hungry! Shari was so full she had trouble with indigestion for a few blocks after leaving until we ran into a street parade. As soon as she heard the music, off she went, dancing even with that bloated sensation in her stomach (she resembled my ninety one year old Mom, who complains that she can't move with her aches and pains. But as soon as she hears music, she's right out there on the floor, dancing). Mike and I also joined in the Samba music, dancing and marching down towards the vendors market at Copacabana beach.

TIP: Don't forget to include antacids when packing medications.

The parade continued on past the vendors market. We stopped there at the vendor's market to make last minute purchases. These later became next to last minute purchases, then next to the next last minute purchases, and so on. "Last minute purchases" didn't end until we finally were on the plane ready for departure. A light drizzly rain had started, but the vendors had their tarps already set up overhead to protect their wares and the customers from the rain. I finished making my purchases, while Shari and Mike continued shopping. Shari kept admonishing me, "Be careful. You are buying too many things. You won't have space for those things in your luggage." At the end, when it was time to leave, guess who had enough space in their luggage for all their last minute purchases, and who didn't (find out in Chapter Ten).

Shari and Mike continued shopping, while I returned to the apartment. But first I made an attempt to say hi, and goodbye, to Ivana. We had not run into her at all since the first night when she shared the ride with us from the airport to our apartment. It seemed that we were always going in a different direction from her hotel, the Savoy Otholon, only two blocks away.

On the plane, Ivana had told me she would be sharing her room at the Savoy Otholon with her good friend, Licha, from the Netherlands, who would arrive Saturday before the Sambadrome competition. Ivana also mentioned that while Licha was her good friend, she still would get upset at her because Licha would steal away all her boyfriends. "Licha doesn't do it for love. She does it for the competition with me," Ivana explained. But still they were good friends. At the front desk of the hotel, I was given Ivana's room number. I also asked for notepaper to leave her a message, in case she wasn't in. Then I took the elevator up to her room on the sixth floor.

The Savoy Otholon doesn't look like much from the outside. In fact, it is located next to a hostel. I expected the hotel to be dumpy though slightly better than the hostel. Instead, the hotel lobby was beautiful, comfortable, and modern. Even the elevator had a futuristic look to it. I easily found Ivana's room, and rang the doorbell.

When the door opened, a drop-dead, breathtaking, tall, beautiful, trim, blondish, gorgeous young woman with sparkling hazel eyes opened the door. She looked at me funny. My shirt and pants were soaked from the rain; my hair, my face, and my arms must have given the impression of a drowned rat. I asked, "Is Ivana in?" She responded, "No, she went out for a while. But she will be back soon. Do you want to come in and wait for her?" I asked, "Are you Licha?" She looked shocked. "How do you know me?" I told her I was on the plane to Rio sitting next to Ivana, and that Ivana told me about her good friend, Licha, from the Netherlands (but I was careful not to mention everything Ivana had told me about her).

Licha invited me again to come in. Instead, I gave her the note I had written and asked her to give it to Ivana. I didn't want to fall into Licha's clutches and have Ivana find me there with Licha in a compromising situation. I had written my email address on the note; Ivana had already given me her email address on the plane. I didn't expect Ivana to email me soon, because in a few days she would begin the next leg of her trip to Buenos Aires, Argentina. Then I returned to my apartment. Shortly thereafter, Shari and Mike also returned, soaked from the rain but cradling their armfuls of "treasures" purchased from shopping the beach vendors.

This is as good a time as any to write about the front door of our apartment.

The front door has two locks, one above the other, that each requires a key to open them. I think I have finally met a door that is more cumbersome to open than the front door of mom's living room. Mom's front door has been missing its door knob handle for close to fifty years (who broke it? "Not me, not me"). Her front door was a custom made, one-of- a-kind door. There was no mass produced hardware to match or replace the broken door handle. I looked for replacement hardware for close to fifteen years, until I finally gave up. To those of us who have lived in that house, the missing doorknob was not a big deal. We know from experience how to open the door without its doorknob, just using the door lock mechanism. Once you know the secret, it opened easily. But for people who don't know about the doorknob, they get perplexed, then flustered, when it came time to open the door to leave.

And so it was with the front door of this apartment. It seemed easy enough to open. Just unlock the top lock, then unlock the bottom lock, then turn the doorknob, and voila, the door should open. Except that… the top lock turned round and around, and you couldn't tell if you were locking, or unlocking, the door. Add to this scenario a bottom lock that needed to be turned at the same time as the door knob for the door to open, and you have a situation where you are alternating hands between the locks and the door knob for minutes at a time until you got lucky and hit the right combination.

Telling this story of the door requires another story, this one about the phone. On our second day there, it sounded like the phone began to ring early in the morning. Shari and Mike were asleep, but I was awake, so I ran from my room into the living room to answer the phone. The phone cradle was empty. Meanwhile, the ringing continued; I couldn't find the receiver. Finally, the ringing stopped. About two days later I heard ringing again in the early morning (about 7:00 am). This time I found the phone receiver, but the room was dark, and I could not see what button to push to talk. By the time I found a light switch, the ringing had stopped.

Today, I heard ringing, again early in the morning. I jumped out of bed, picked up the receiver, and responded, "Hello, Hello." But there was no answer. I started hitting every button on the receiver, trying to get a response, and continuing to say, "Hello, hello," but still no answer. Meanwhile, the incessant ringing continued. Finally, Mike yelled out from his bed, "It's the front door. Open the door!"

I realized now that it was the doorbell I had been hearing those other mornings, not the phone. Mike's set of keys were in both the locks on the door, so it seemed to be a simple enough maneuver. I tried turning the top lock around and around. Even with the clattering of the sets of keys in each lock I couldn't get that right combination, and the door stayed locked. The buzzing continued. I shouted out, "Un momento." Then I heard someone on the other side of the door say something in Portuguese, but I didn't understand what they were saying. Meanwhile, the incessant buzzing continued. I kept turning both locks, trying to get the right combination to open the door. Then I heard keys on the other side of the door.

I realized that whomever was on the other side of the door probably knew how to open the door. As they were opening the locks from the outside, I must have been relocking them on the inside. I stopped, and within moments, the door opened. It was the maid, coming in to perform cleaning and to wash our laundry.

Chapter Nine

FAREWELL TO RIO

Wednesday, February 6, 2008

How fast time passes when you are having fun! Today was the last day of our trip to Rio. Late tonight we will catch our shuttle back to Galeao International for the flight out at 4:00 am in the morning. But we still had a big portion of today to experience more of Brazil. I was the first one up, so I made coffee. Shari heard my rustle in the kitchen and got up shortly afterwards. Today, Shari's eyes were open wider than they had been all day yesterday, after getting home at 6:00 am from the Sambadrome. Yesterday her eyes were just slits barely open; she had an Asian look to her. But today her eyes only look dazed. Mike stayed asleep.

It had rained all through the night. The noisy and boisterous crowd finally quieted around 4:00 am. Today is Ash Wednesday. No more Carnaval until next year. As I looked down at the street from my window, many thoughts came to me.

View of street below from apartment window

I don't consider myself a sheltered person, but it has actually been fun for me to look out the window each day at the street below. So much has happened.

I've witnessed some of the ugliness of Rio, but also much of the good it offers. For several days I have watched the shopkeeper in the alley across the street as he swept his patio free of debris every day, several times a day. I've watched people drunk on the street. I've seen numerous people go through the trash containers outside on the street looking for aluminum cans. I've watched people of all ages coming and going down the street on their daily business. I've watched children skipping down the street, and a bicycle being ridden over what I thought was a drunk man sleeping off his previous night's partying. I've watched people in the apartments across the way leaning out of their windows for a few minutes each day to see the activity below; it's like they look out to see what the day has in store for them, then they lose interest and leave their window sill empty. It was shocking to hear Brazilians say, "Urno Shakesnaker" when we would tell them we were from California. Our governor at that time (Arnold Schwarzenegger) had a very strong public presence in Brazil. "Disneyland" was no longer the face of California in their minds.

Something I had not mentioned earlier was the favela (a slum) behind the apartments across the street from us. The favela was barely perceptible to us, but was distinguishable because it had a different look from the apartments. This favela was one of many favelas throughout the city. Actually, the favelas housed more people than those who live in apartments. Although the apartments tower into the sky, the favelas rose above and behind them up the mountainsides.

When I inquired about visiting a favela to see it up close, I was told, "Tourists are not welcome in favelas! Best to stay out of them, or you may run into trouble!"

A favela, the reddish structures on the upper right side
of the center apartment

The apartments are painted in pretty colors and have A/C units hanging outside on the window sills; the favelas are constructed of red brick, with their exterior walls having a moldy appearance. Many of the favela units have large blue containers in the back (to catch water?) and blue tarps overhead (to cover holes in the roofs from the rain?). At night you can see a sea of TV screens from both the apartments and the favelas. The two or three Brazilian TV stations are what seem to keep the country united, because everyone knows the same news, the same problems, and the same direction the country is taking.

Mike got up. Although his hair was standing straight up and disheveled, and his eyes barely open to slits, he looked alive and ready to dance, if only he could get a little more sleep.

Our plan for today was to stay in out of the rain by visiting an indoor mall, where we could shop for more "last minute purchases." After taking a bus to De Vassa, and eating a buffet lunch there, we walked to the indoor mall, which was a short distance away. However, many of the shops were closed, possibly for siesta time.

In all of his readings prior to the trip, Mike had read about H. Stern Jewelers, whose international headquarters were located here in Rio.H.Stern has a worldwide reputation for its jewelry settings. It manufactured jewelry on the premises. Shari had wanted a different setting for her wedding ring for some time. Mike felt this might be a good opportunity to have her ring reset. Both he and Shari wanted to visit the business to see what could be done.

Conveniently, the H.Stern headquarters were in the same neighborhood as the mall. The general public is welcome to tour the business.

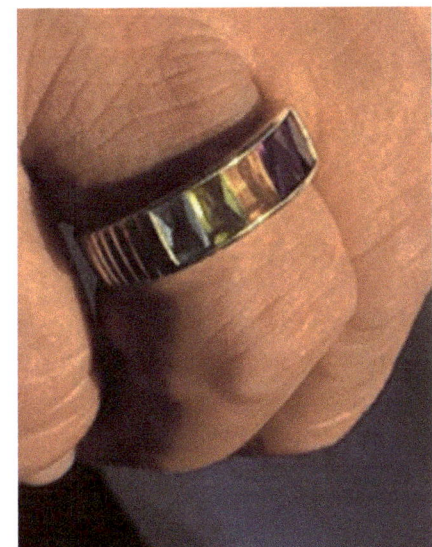

This international headquarters of H.Stern is very impressive. It was a first class experience. You are greeted at the door of a three story building, given a tour of the various manufacturing areas where we could watch jewelry being made from scratch, given refreshments (including small alcoholic drinks if requested), and, of course, given a sales pitch. Unfortunately, H.Stern did not perform the resetting of stones. They are in the business of creating settings for new stones.

A young saleswoman, named Wang, showed us some of the beautiful jewelry individually manufactured on premises. She was mainly displaying women's rings, but then I inquired about rings for men. She brought out four trays of men's rings. One ring in particular caught my eye. It was a ring of five stones, including (and symbolizing) blue Topaz ("Protection"), Peridot ("Happiness"), Citrine ("Wealth"), Amethyst ("Health"), and Garnet ("Love"). It was an 18K gold ring, 3.15 carats. I decided to buy this ring as a symbol of a new beginning and a new chapter in my life.

At the end of the tour, a limo gave all the guests a free ride back to their hotel (or, in our case, our apartment). Rather than ride a bus back in the rain, we were taken in a limo (a Mercedes Benz passenger van).

Out of the nine main things we had planned to do on this trip to Rio, we accomplished six. The others (including a tour of Botafogo Bay, Candelaria Church, Fiscal Island, the Tujuca Forest, the botanical gardens, and many other sights) were not accomplished because we ran out of time, or we were resting, or our body clocks weren't yet in sync, or it was raining. But we did accomplish other things not on the list which added to our experience the Brazilian pizza, the churrasco, the kilograma, drinking caipirinha, shopping the vendor's markets along the beaches of Copacabana and Ipanema, and visiting H.Stern headquarters.

My only regret was that by being sick, I was unable to fully enjoy the party atmosphere of Carnaval. Also, I was unable to spend several hours sitting on the beach at Copacabana or Ipanema for any stretch of time on a sunny day soaking in the rays of the sun and getting "pink." I will have to make another trip back someday just to do this.

Chapter Ten

PANAMA CITY

Thursday, February 7, 2008

Now that the nights were quiet, we made every attempt in the early evening to try to catch up on sleep, but we were too excited about packing, and the last minute details that needed attention. Our driver picked us up at 12:30 am to take us to Galeao International Airport for our return flight to LAX via a layover in Panama City.

The layover in Panama City would have duration of about eight hours. The only thing I thought that might be of interest to me in Panama was the Panama Canal. But I was wrong. In the short eight hours we spent here, I had the equivalent of at least four days of fun packed into one day. Too bad that I was so tired. I could barely enjoy it.

First, on the flight from Rio to Panama City, I was seated next to Laura and Brock, a young couple from Sydney, Australia, whose destination was Cancun. The airlines we were using for the first leg of our return (COPA Airlines) didn't have a direct flight from Rio to Cancun. Instead, COPA booked them from Rio through Panama City where they would change planes with us. From there, the flight would take them to Los Angeles, then, from Los Angeles, back to Mexico City, and from there, to Cancun. When Laura and Brock found out that they could have booked a direct flight to Cancun from Rio using different airline carriers, they were extremely upset not only because of the delay in time, but also the increased cost. As a young couple, they didn't know any better when hassling the flight arrangements with the ticket agent. And, they did not have a command of the Portuguese language, or the know-how with which to make inquiries at the airport, like our in-house guide, Mike.

They were a very nice couple. I had noticed Laura at the airport check-in counter in Rio mainly because she was wearing a dress that I can only describe as a halter top miniskirt. She had very nice, long, slender tanned legs. I had also noticed her and Brock at the departure counter because it appeared that they were having some sort of problem, and it looked like they reluctantly turned away from the counter upset at something. It turned out it was the flight booking problem to Cancun that they were upset with. If I would have known it then, I would have mentioned it to our in-house guide, Mike, so he could go over to assist them; he is always willing to lend assistance when approached.

When we reached Panama City, we had already decided ahead of time to tour the city rather that just sit in the airport terminal waiting, as in the Fantasy Island TV show, for "da plane, da plane" (e.g., our transfer plane).

TIP: Use long periods of wait to sight-see; otherwise, you are "losing" experiences.

Our checked luggage would automatically be loaded into the new plane bound for Los Angeles. But now Shari and Mike had armfuls of bags with carry-on purchases (all their "treasures" from the Rio street vendors that didn't fit into their luggage). These were bulky, loose, and too heavy to be carrying all day throughout the city. I only had my back pack to carry, and it was too small to hold all their bags. Mike's thought was to rent a locker at the airport to store their bags of carry-on items. At this airport, though, there were no lockers. We went into a luggage sales shop to inquire if there was a place we could leave the carry- on bags, but were told there was no such place in this airport. Somehow, it came out that while this shop could not hold a traveler's excess bags, if a piece of luggage in that shop were purchased, the store could hold that piece of luggage until the buyer returned to pick it up. This had to all be done on the same day (e.g., purchase a piece of luggage, then pick it up later the same day).

I have had my same luggage for about ten years, and have found that an oversize (not the normal size) rolling duffel bag would be very helpful for my needs.

It could replace one small suitcase and a regular size duffel bag which, even when combined together, doesn't give me enough room for my things. With this in mind, I looked more closely at the duffel bags offered in this luggage shop. I found an oversized rolling bag that would provide multipurpose uses for my future needs. I purchased it, let Shari and Mike put their bags of treasures in it, and lightened my own backpack load as well. Then the shop clerk allowed me to leave the now full, newly purchased, duffel bag there at the shop for pickup later in the day.

As the cashier was ringing up my purchase, she inquired, "What do you have planned for today?" Here in Panama, the official language was Spanish; now I could converse without having to use the in-house interpreter (Mike). Shari and I responded that we were going to tour the city, using taxis and buses. We wanted to see the Panama Canal, but we also wanted to see any other points of interest in the city. The cashier told us that her husband was a taxi driver, and that he gave tours of the city. If we were interested, she would call him and arrange for him to take us around the city for the day. This sounded good to us. It fit right into our plans; we agreed. She called her husband, and we arranged a spot outside the terminal, and a time, where he could pick us up at the airport. First, though, we had to clear customs, then find an ATM.

At Customs we were asked to present our tourist cards. Up to now, no one had mentioned any need of a tourist card. But a little booth off to the side had tourist cards for sale for five dollars US (Panamanian currency was the same value as US dollars); it was only a short delay to purchase them and fill them out. Then we headed for the exit. The airport did not have an ATM.

Panama is making every effort to preserve its history

Gustavo, the taxi driver, was already at the exit waiting for us. He had a sign with Mike's name written on it. Gustavo spoke "Panamanian Spanish" (e.g., a mixture of Spanish and Portuguese). Since Shari and I both speak Spanish, this gave Mike a much needed break from translation responsibilities. Gustavo agreed to give us a tour of the city for sixty dollars. This sounded reasonable to us. By law, Panamanian currency, particularly coinage, had to be equal in size, facial value, weight and metallic content as that of the USA.

Needless to say, this tour was an excellent investment of our time and money.

Gustavo was very eager, very patient, he stayed close to us (which served as a deterrent to the locals to leave us alone, including people asking for a donation of money), and he explained things as he was driving (and driving in a manner only cab drivers can do in and out of traffic). He answered our questions, and gave his own personal commentary about things, such as that every street corner in Panama City has its own "Mu Dono's" (McDonald's restaurant); it sure seemed that he was right. He mentioned that parents had to cover their children's eyes when passing Mu Dono's, otherwise the children would rant and rave about stopping, not to eat, but to play in the McDonald's playground.

Gustavo's taxi dashboard had a little religious statue that I didn't recognize, so I asked him about it. He told me it was the statue of the "Black Christ," his patron saint.

The Black Christ had helped a famous Panamanian personality recover from alcoholism and drug abuse, so Gustavo, who is a black Panamanian, made this his own personal religious icon to keep him out of harm's way. Gustavo was very impressed and proud to say that Mel Gipson and Brad Pitt were famous in Panama and had purchased much land here.

There was a particular restaurant Mike had read about in his travel guide that he wanted to try, Restaurante Cedro's. It was located in the old Panama City (the New Panama City of high rise buildings and commerce was where the "rich people" live and work across the bay). Gustavo did not recognize the restaurant or its location. He kept stopping to ask bystanders for the street that the restaurant was located on. He kept going around and around in large circles. I asked him if Panamanians give directions like some nationalities do – everyone has a different version of where something is located ("Over there; a few blocks further down; keep going; turn left; turn right," etc). Gustavo grudgingly agreed.

We finally found the restaurant. It wasn't yet open for lunch; it was only 11:00 am. We walked around the old city to pass the time. We went into an ancient looking church in the center of the old city (La Iglesia de Los Pobres). The interior is very spacious upwards in height towards the ceiling, but down below has narrow pews and aisles, and rickety wooden benches. The church was built in the 1500's, when Spain began to colonize the New World. The art inside was a mixture of three dimensional porcelain and wood carvings/ sculptures, with paintings/images of the church's bishops for over five hundred years. This church must have served as the main headquarters of the Spanish Catholic church in the New World throughout the years of Spanish colonization.

Inside the church there was a small shop selling religious goods. Outside the church are the historic streets of old Panama City. Part of this historic area was currently in use as a movie set for the James Bond movie that would be released at the end of 2008. At the edge of the old city was the location of the former Spanish garrison, which housed the soldiers in the 1500's and 1600's protecting the city from pirates, in particular, "El pirate, Morgan."

The garrison also housed the prison, which has now been turned into a fancy restaurant. Its history was brutal. We saw a real ball and chain used through the centuries on prisoners. I lifted it; it was very heavy. A person in a weakened state would not be able to escape if shackled. As a form of torture, the Spaniards would starve their prisoners, then string them up inside the dining room to watch the military officers dine. There was an outside cage adjacent to the dining room where prisoners would be left to rot from the effects of heat and sun exposure; then the buzzards would be let in to finish off whatever remained of the prisoners, dead or alive. If the prison was too full, "excess" prisoners would be shoved out of another barred room into the bay for the sharks to finish them off. I felt I had to say a prayer for all those prisoners who perished under these conditions. I could not understand how this could now be a fancy restaurant, where people actually wanted to eat and enjoy their food. Maybe they were unaware of its past. I was sickened to my stomach thinking of the past atrocities committed here.

Having an interest in history, the background of piracy at Panama City was most interesting to me. The pirate, Morgan, was the most famous of the pirates who terrorized and pillaged the city. As the center of Spanish influence, the gold and silver collected in the New World on the Pacific Ocean side would accumulate in Panama City to be transported via ship to Spain. To discourage rebellion from the natives, and open battles on city streets, a secret tunnel had been built under the city streets (probably using forced labor) to transfer accumulated wealth from a fortified area inside the city to waiting Spanish ships off shore.

Unable to be seen from above, the tunnel (in the center where the sand meets the rock) has been sealed

But, of course, the pirates found out about the "secret passage way". There was another way the pirates could locate the accumulated treasures. An obelisk had been constructed on the main square to serve as a sun dial.

At a certain time of the day, the obelisk would cast a shadow that served as a line-of-sight to the repository. Once these two secrets were out, pirate raids became more frequent. Looking at the layout of the old city, and the garrison position next to the ocean, it was easy to imagine pitched battles between the pirates and the Spanish soldiers in the streets and in the tunnel. These scenarios sure helped make Indiana Jones movies more vivid.

The old Panama City had narrow brick (cobblestone type) streets, with two or three story apartment buildings that all had iron railing window patios, similar to what is seen in movies, or even at the "Pirates of the Caribbean" ride at Disneyland. It reinforced the image of raiding and fighting for treasure in the city streets, and of females standing at the railings throwing kisses to their protectors or to the adventurous raiders.

After a tour of the former Spanish garrison/prison, we walked back to Cedro's Restaurant.

We were hungry. Since we were now in a different setting, thoughts of the horrors we had just heard about vanished. We enjoyed a delicious lunch of chicken, rice mixed with black beans, potato salad, and vegetables, all prepared "Panamanian style." There were other meat entrées, but I wasn't about to take a chance on eating something unknown, so I stayed with what I could see was something I recognized. At first glance, the chicken looked like a small portion; it ended up providing a lot of meat. Gustavo joined us for lunch, courtesy of Mike. He finished his lunch before Shari and Mike made it to the table with their food selections, and went outside to wait for us.

After lunch, Gustavo drove us to the Panama Canal administration building located at the Mira Flores locks. The administration building housed the museum showing the canal being constructed, a gift shop, an informational video of ten minutes (which was lost on us as we fell asleep in no time in the comfortable padded chairs in the air conditioned theater), and a place to observe the locks in action.

The museum had several levels to it. At the end of the first level I was too tired to continue on. I sat down inside the lobby to wait for Shari and Mike to finish their tour of the museum. Thankfully, there were no "new treasures" collected by them from this museum. Meanwhile, there was a public announcement that a cargo ship was now in the lock; I went outside to watch. Gustavo, who had joined me inside on the bench, also went outside with me to watch.

I felt hungry again. There was a snack shop outside where I bought a couple of beers and some empanadas (little breads stuffed with meat) for me, as well as some for Gustavo (he wanted soda rather than beer, since he was the driver). When we first arrived at Mira Flores, it was sunny and humid outside.

While we were in the theater, there was a downpour of heavy rain, followed by excessive heat and humidity. It still wasn't as hot or humid as in Rio.

Finally, Shari and Mike emerged, and Gustavo took us back to the airport via the long way, right through the middle of the city (rather than using the freeway). We were able to see the former US military base, and observed the local people, local types of stores, homes, and apartments. We experienced the local driving conditions, and even followed behind the local "Red Devil buses." Gustavo commented, "No one, neither pedestrian nor vehicle, challenges the Red Devil buses for right of way!"

Finally, we were back at the airport with plenty of time before the flight out. We asked Gustavo what we owed him for his outstanding service. He just shrugged his shoulders, and didn't reply. We had included him in our lunch, and bought him refreshments. We had peppered him with questions and treated him like he was important as we traveled through the city. Mike and I made sure he was well compensated for his efforts. We gave him almost double his original asking price.

Chapter Eleven

EPILOGUE

Now that our trip to Rio was over, what was my impression of Rio, and how did I enjoy the trip? Was it worth the money spent, and risking my health to go? Well, when we arrived in Rio in the late evening hours, it looked bleak like the homeless area of downtown Los Angeles. People were sleeping on the sidewalks under blankets; some people sleeping didn't have blankets. The streets looked dark and creepy. Scrounged people and ugly women seemed to be everywhere. Trash was piled up as high and as far as you could see.

But after dancing in the street parades and witnessing the Samba competition, now I want to go back! The Samba music spoke to my soul! In the daylight the city is beautiful. I can picture myself living there and enjoying the ambiance, the beer, the food, the beautiful women, and the beach (if it ever stops raining). During daylight hours, the people do not appear ugly or creepy looking. Cristo Redentor, and Sugarloaf, were spectacular.

I loved seeing canopies of trees lining the streets, and providing coolness from the heat.

Rio has the best of, and the life of, other major international cities. Its round-the-clock beat matches Las Vegas. It has as many nationalities represented as New York City. It has the traffic of Mexico City. It has the homeless people living on the streets like in Los Angeles. It has the hills and trees of San Francisco. It has the rain of Seattle.

Rio has an infrastructure I am accustomed to. The streets are well paved, and maintained. The street signage was clear and easy to read, though there were times when I didn't understand how the street directional indicators could be "green" for me to travel in one direction, yet cars passing in the cross direction thought they had the right of way. Except for trash nights, there was very little evidence of litter.

The shop keepers go to great lengths to ensure their little kingdom of property was kept clean by being swept several times daily. I did not step on anyone's bubble gum left on the sidewalk during the entire trip.

Although the streets were crowded with cars, which were zooming into every little open space on the street that presented itself, there were very few fender benders, mainly because the cars were being driven slower. There was no apparent problem with communications – the TV stations and phone service seemed to operate in good working order. Internet cable seemed readily available. Water from the tap was said to be ok to drink, but was supposedly so heavily chlorinated that it tasted terrible. Water pressure was one thing that I wasn't thrilled with. Sometimes, when showering, the hot water level would drop momentarily, then the pressure would resume with cold water for a few moments before returning to the original heat level. But I have experienced this same problem here in my own home, so this type of problem was not limited to Brazil.

I was surprised with the honesty of the local people. On the subway, a young woman approached Shari to ask if this was Shari's first time in Rio. She advised Shari to remove her neck jewelry (a crucifix on a gold chain) because it could provide someone a temptation to steal it from her. And, in a street parade, I had young people who were concerned about my backpack, giving me hints about how easily it could be opened, and the contents stolen. The locals were as concerned for me as they were for Shari, or would be for any tourist.

Rio is a vibrant city that moves with, and breathes, the musical soul of Brazil. Samba is a music that reaches the innermost recesses of your soul, and makes you come alive.

Do I want to make a return visit? My bags can be packed within minutes, and I am ready to catch a flight back right now! Next time, though, I hope to travel healthy!

Pancho, the crazy Huntington Beach Senior
Apartments White Devil Bus Driver

95

Sambadrome Competition

(Examples of 60+ floats and 75+ sections of dancers)

www.ingramcontent.com/pod-product-compliance
Lightning Source LLC
Chambersburg PA
CBHW051541120626
46551CB00013B/1319